GODMADE
MEN

Copyright © 2019 Ryan Andrews

All rights reserved.

Published in the United States by DreamSurf Studio Publishing. Except as permitted under the United States Copyright Act of 1976, no part of this publication may be reproduced or distributed in any form or by any means, or stored in a database or retrieval system, without prior written permission by the publisher.

Andrews, Ryan
GODMADE MEN
/ Ryan Andrews – 1st ed.

ISBN 978-0-9983068-2-7
Printed in the United States of America

Design by DreamSurf Studio

FIRST EDITION

I dedicate this book to the love of my life Nissa and my children. You mean more to me than life itself. I am in awe of who you are and that God chose me to be your champion.

To my sons, Ezekiel, Luke, and Micah - learn to be Godmade men and walk in His truth all the days of your lives. Find a Godmade wife, and raise Godmade children.

For my beautiful daughter Glory, search for a man who built his life in God. Learn how to be a Godmade woman. And how to raise Godmade children.

Thank you, my family, for loving me through the rough spots on my journey to become the man that God has called me to be.

CONTENTS

GODMADE MAN
00 A Note To Men — 5
01 Created For More — 8
02 How Did I Get Here — 18
03 Father of Fathers — 32
04 Jesus Is The Example — 42
05 God Is The List — 50
06 True Lies — 60

GODMADE HUSBAND
07 Winning Her Heart — 70
08 Men Of Action — 78
09 The Secret Weapon (The Sex Chapter) — 86
10 Champion — 96

GODMADE DAD
11 This Changes Everything — 104
12 Dad Failures — 116
13 The Sacrificial Dad — 130
14 I Believe In You — 142

WE ARE GODMADE
15 Unbroken — 154
16 The Change — 162
–> **My Gift To You** — 173

A NOTE TO MEN

The self-made man is killing us, wounding our children and destroying marriages. A self-made man is one whom has learned to be self sufficient and has fought hard to become the man he wanted to be. He has struggled without the support of others to build himself. The self-made man earns his place by blood sweat and tears. This man is always striving even once successful.

One day, he will look in the mirror many years from the beginning of that struggle only to have left a wake of wounded people in his path. The disconnection from his family almost complete, he is unsure of his own passions and dreams. That man has created a life motivated by fear. The fear of not measuring up, not having what it takes, and not having respect. Whatever the underlying struggle may be, the self-made man has a measure of success in some areas of his life at the expense of others.

The Godmade man overflows with life. His family loves to be around him, his relationships are strong and healthy, he is successful in business, and is continually being filled to overflow. The Godmade man is solid in his identity, never questions his own worth, and is motivated by love. One day he will look in the mirror after many years of thriving to see a life of peace, full of freedom and empowering those under his cover.

I was a self-made man, successful on the outside but a complete mess on the inside. We lived in Hawaii, with our three kids, owned rental property, and I worked for myself from home. Externally a perfect life, but inside I was dying everyday. I just wanted to run away and hide. Being a good self-made man I learned how to sacrifice my own wellbeing to be home and work hard. My health suffered, my work suffered, my wife and kids suffered, and I was building a perfect life that would likely end in divorce and emotional pain.

I'm writing this book because my soul awakened to being the man that God made me to be. I've learned how to champion my wife to her greatness, and why it's a biblical call. I've learned how to be myself with my kids and still have them think I'm a superhero. My marriage went from being ok to great, and my kids have told me how happy they are with the new me.

Many of the beliefs about what a man is supposed to be come from generational habits more than biblical truths. Even though I was surrounded by Godly men it was difficult to find the freedom that I now have. From accountability groups to mens meetings I heard the same thing; self-control. We are supposed to control who we are to fit a mold. The teaching around sin is all messed up.

Men are good. We are told by modern media and even sometimes the church that men need to behave differently, that we're inept, and if only we could be more like women then we can get their approval. But, that isn't what God says.

I have felt my whole life like the world hates me because I'm a man. I've heard from the pulpit that men need to be softer, more like Jesus. But I'm not soft. I'm more of a mix between Peter and King David. By the way, Jesus wasn't soft either.

I am writing this book because my life has gone from normal to insanely awesome ever since my awakening, and it's time to let my brothers in on the secret. My wife is excited to be with me, my kids can't wait to see me, and I can't wait to be with them. We all need down time and alone time, but what I discovered about connection and my wants versus my needs has revolutionized the way we connect as a family. It's time to be Godmade men instead of the self-made idiot that the world thinks we are. It's never too late to become the man that God created us to be.

JOIN THE COMMUNITY ON FACEBOOK
facebook.com/groups/godmademen

CHAPTER 1
CREATED FOR MORE

I CAME THAT THEY MAY HAVE LIFE,
AND HAVE IT ABUNDANTLY.
JOHN 10:10

No more lies. It's time for radical honesty. I was dying inside and I didn't know why. I blamed my health, wife, kids, job, bills, or anything else because I wasn't able to be completely honest.

The self-made man is killing us, wounding our children and destroying marriages. The truth is that we are so far from the man that God created us to be that we don't even know what it looks like. We do our best to show up and be the best version that we can. Following in the footsteps of self-made men that have come before seems to be our best option.

Then, every once in awhile we meet a man who shows that God created us for more. I call them Godmade men. They are guys just like us that have let God be the one that builds their life instead of their experiences. Usually they seem to have a good work life balance, their kids are doing well, they are successful, and their marriage makes some jealous. They are the shining example of an abundant life.

Take a moment and think about how it would feel to have every area of life in complete abundance. What if there was an abundant flow happening right now. Imagine your finances overflowing in a way that allows you to live in freedom. You are able to give freely to everyone who needs, and there is no lack in your house. Selah (pause and reflect).

Breathing that in and out feels really good. Now, imagine that you are living in the marriage of your dreams. If you're not married, you've met the perfect woman and she is everything that you desire. If you are married, your wife is overflowing with love every time she sees you. Her heart is so full of passion for you that she is excited to see you every time you come home. She constantly believes in you and even when you fail she is right there to support you through it without fear of judgment. She respects you with every fiber of her being. What does that feel like? Selah.

It takes a powerful man to follow his heart calling. No one is more attractive than one who is fully alive to their purpose. What would your life look like if you were pursuing your passion? What would it look like if you felt completely alive to your purpose? Do you even know what that is? I didn't.

If you're in a similar place to where I was then it might be difficult to imagine a life that isn't full of striving. I would have been happy to just have less stress. If the bills got paid on time, and my family was mostly happy then it would have felt like a huge win. And that's the problem. We believe that an average life is the best that we can hope for.

God didn't create some men great and others to be worker bees. We were all created with one purpose in mind, to commune with God on a deep intimate level. The base of our destiny is to be like all the great men of faith that we've ever read about. Anything less than living an abundant life is falling short of our destiny.

Here is an adaptation from proverbs thirty one that represents a snap shot of what one Godmade man might look like. I believe that everyone has a calling in their heart that could be written out in a format similar to this. Let these words sink in for a minute.

THE PROVERBIAL MAN
(adapted from Proverbs 31)

The perfect man who can find?

His value is far above gold.

The heart of his wife believes in him and he excels in all areas of wealth.

He raises his family up and does not cause strife.

He looks for ways to increase in business and like a rising tide floats all ships around him.

His day starts early and prepares his household to grow.

He invests in generational wealth building and also increases in fitness and personal health.

He knows that his gain is built through God's plan and is full of energy which carries him through long nights with ease.

He is generous and has a place in his life for those in need.

He is an important part of leading his family into their spiritual calling.

He is an example of what it means to be a child of God the Father.

He wears his reputation like fine clothing.

He champions his wife's dreams, and important people know her value because of it.

They, together, are a place of inner abundance to those around them.

He is slow to speak and quick to listen, and when he does speak it is full of wisdom and not strife.

His children and wife respect him and their love for him is apparent to everyone who looks.

His wife praises him saying, "Many sons have done well but you excel them all."

Even though he is charming and well dressed, it is his fear of the Lord that people most praise.

Give him anything to do and his works will speak for themselves, raising the respect of those in the world for him.

DESTINY

The word destiny can feel a bit out of reach. Like having a dream to one day own a professional sports team. Talking about destiny can cause some pressure to try to make something happen so, I'll do my best to bring it down to the realm of possibility.

Destiny is not our future. It is not a fate that supersedes free will. Destiny is who we are in the present as God sees us.

We were created with unique gifts and characteristics. God calls us to move toward the life that best suits who we are at our core. He knows us better than we know ourselves. It is our honor and task to learn how to align who we believe that we are with how God knows us.

Whenever I write about destiny, understand that I'm speaking about stepping into who we already are. Our behaviors do not impact Godly identity. If you're messing things up now, it doesn't change how God sees you. God is love, and love always believe the best.

It is the destiny of every man to be a great leader, husband

and father. Whether we're a spiritual father or a natural father, a leader to nations or a small team at work, greatness is what we were designed for. The call that echoes in all of our hearts is to discover the fullness of the power that God put in our DNA.

VISION

One great exercise that I use frequently is creating a vision for my life. We practiced a little of it earlier in this chapter. The basic concept is that without a clear and detailed vision for the life that we want to have it will be impossible to flourish. Every leader must have a personal vision for the people they are in charge of.

Creating a vision takes some practice to be completely honest with what we want, so it's valuable to keep a vision fluid. The main components of a viable vision is that it's no longer than three years from today, and it creates positive feelings when thinking about the outcome.

I always start with a dream that seems really far off. Dream big and think about things that seem outside the realm of possibility. Then I move on to what would be good to accomplish in the next three years that could move me toward the big dream.

Here's the key to it all; feel it. Close your eyes and think about what it would feel like to achieve each part of that vision. If the vision is owning a bed and breakfast business then think about sitting in your office running that company. What kind of mug are you drinking your coffee from? How many staff members do you have? What city is it in? Go into detail and really envision yourself in that place.

Do this for every area of your life. Really take the time to feel it, think about things, and envision them as a reality. What does it feel like?

Now, what would if feel like if three years from today nothing changes? What does it feel like if you're in the same financial situation, your relationships and family situations are the same. What if nothing more is accomplished? How would that feel?

If you're anything like me then it would feel like a waste of life. Here's the thing, three years are going to come and go one way or the other. There is never a better time than today to fulfill the calling in your heart. Write the vision down clearly and with the intention of using it as a guide to run toward destiny.

> Record the vision and inscribe it on tablets,
> that the one who reads it may run.
> -Habakkuk 2:2

RADICAL HONESTY

I was a good man, and I loved Jesus. I was a worship pastor, and I read my bible inconsistently; but I did spend time in the word. Yet, I was dying inside. I prophesied, prayed for the sick and saw some healings. I went on missions trips, and lead others into an encounter with God. But the fruit of a deep spiritual connection was not there.

To be perfectly honest, back then I felt like I was doing all the right stuff. Looking back now though, I can see that I was so far from having a close relationship with God that I still feel like repenting.

It's time for some radical honesty. How connected do you feel with God? Is it a 24/7 relationship where even in your sleep your spirit man is hanging out with Him? If you were to rate how much of His will is present in your life on a scale of 1 to 10, where does it land?

This is a challenge to have a truly honest internal conversation. Even now for myself I feel like there are times where I might answer 10 and other times where I might struggle to say 5. There is no shame or judgment in whatever response is there for you. It's a call to be internally aware. If things need to improve, then do the work.

I'm not sure what came first, a strong connection with my wife or a strong connection with God. What I do know, is that one definitely supports the other. A man with a strong connection to his wife will also have a strong connection to God. And a man that fears the Lord openly will have an amazing marriage.

Apply the same radical honesty to your relationships, how you show up at work, and how well you take care of your body. Are you fulfilling the call on your life? Take the time to work out the answers to these questions with one important thing in mind. You were designed by God for greatness.

WHAT DOES IT LOOK LIKE?

If, we were made with unique gifts and callings, and we were made for a time such as this to shine brightly, then what does it look like? I call it, life by design. Whether it was designed by us, or by the Lord is the only real question. By not stepping into our destiny we are forwarding the plans of the enemy. Looking back, I can see how small my impact was, compared to what it is now.

What if my children grew up to resent me and walk away from God because I couldn't curb my anger? What if my wife had enough of me and left? I could tell you now that I wouldn't have landed in a good place. All the stuff that I was doing "for God" was for nothing if I couldn't fulfill my calling as a husband and father.

First Corinthians chapter thirteen is known as the love chapter, and it starts with, "If I were to speak with eloquence in earth's many languages, and in the heavenly tongues of angels, yet I didn't express myself with love, my words would be reduced to the hollow sound of nothing more than a clanging cymbal.

And if I were to have the gift of prophecy with a profound understanding of God's hidden secrets, and if I possessed unending supernatural knowledge, and if I had the greatest gift of faith that could move mountains, but have never learned to love, then I am nothing.

And if I were to be so generous as to give away everything I owned to feed the poor, and to offer my body to be burned as a martyr, without the pure motive of love, I would gain nothing of value." *(The Passion Translation)*

God's call for us begins and ends with Love. If the people we are closest to don't feel loved because of how stressed we are, then what good is the rest of our actions.

A life by God's design is one that is full of Agape love. Our family feels the weighty glory of our love, and we cover them in it like a warm blanket. The fruit of a Godmade man is pure love.

Since most of the men I meet are still learning how to keep on loving even when it hurts, including myself, I'm going to assume that you are still not walking in the fullness of what God has for you. Here's the great news, there are no requirements for what your life looks like. God is interested in what you want, and many of the burning desires in your heart were placed there by him to lead you into greatness.

What does your life look like in its perfect form? If there were no limitations, and you could have anything, and be anything, and live anywhere, how would it go? Take time right now to get a picture of the perfect Godmade life. How does it feel? We're going to do this exercise again at the end of the book because a good vision is stepped through multiple times until it lands in the perfect place of our heart. Know that God is on your side, and He's rooting for you to win!

> I am created for greatness not mediocrity.

CHAPTER 2

HOW DID I GET HERE

THE LUKEWARM DON'T EVEN
KNOW THEY ARE DYING.
REV 3:17

Not too many years ago sitting in a café working on the computer a deep sense of misery hit hard. I had been on an unknown downward spiral for many years but learned to ignore all signs of depression like a good little Christian should. At that time, my wife and I had three kids and were living in Hawaii. I worked for myself, she took care of the children, and I was the worship pastor at our church. We owned rental property, and for all intents and purposes, we had a perfect life; except that I was miserable. It wouldn't be until years later that we found out she was unhappy too, but that's for later on in the story.

I felt trapped by my own life. I loved my kids, but they were so hard to deal with. It felt as though I would be better with them when they're older. If I could just make it through this little kid phase, then it will be my time to shine. I loved my wife, but getting some action was a touchy subject. We had a good sex life according to most, but often I felt more like she was doing me a favor than us actually enjoying connecting with each other physically.

Being the sole breadwinner, there was a self-imposed added pressure to make sure that everyone was taken care of financially. Except, I didn't have a clue what I was doing. I kept my mouth shut and worked hard. If I made enough money, then maybe it wouldn't matter except money was tight, so now add financial failure to the list of mounting self esteem issues.

My wife was amazing, she really was. We never fought, the kids were well taken care of and the house was always in order. She loved Jesus and was so much more spiritual than me. Sure, I was the worship pastor, but if anyone knew how much I struggled then I would probably have been kicked out of church. At least this is how it felt, a perfect wife and kids, and then the loser in the mirror.

I had learned how to be positive and seemed like a happy guy. And for the most part, I was a happy person. It's mostly because men are good at compartmentalizing our emotions, so I could still show up as the life of the party when needed.

It wasn't obvious that I was miserable. I didn't realize that until the moment in the cafe. I think most of us don't spend time thinking about what's going on inside. We just know that what's going on outside isn't great.

I yelled a lot. That's sign number one that something needs to change. When I say, "something" I mean, me. I acted like the external stuff was making me angry. Except changing all the external stuff wouldn't resolve the belief inside that I wasn't good enough and was potentially one misstep away from being found out.

Through the 10 years of marriage to this point, I was leading worship every Sunday, prayed often, and even read my bible from time to time. I went to conferences, had rad God encounters, and was connected to great mentors. I was not spiritually devoid, and yet what I was doing didn't seem to make a difference in my life, our marriage or the kids.

I remember one time having a neighbor come by and check on us. I was all bark, so everyone was ok physically. But, I have a loud bark and don't have much "fear of man" issues, so everyone in the whole neighborhood knew when I wasn't happy. How embarrassing for my family. (Neighbors, if you're reading this. Sorry for being a jerk, everyone is much happier now.)

Everything that I'm writing about was subtle. It was a bunch of little things adding up. We had fun days at the beach and I had good months financially. My wife and I have always been great at talking, so date night was usually fun. From the outside there didn't seem like any crisis was happening.

Once the realization hit that I couldn't go on living like this and something needed to change, then everything seemed like a problem. I avoided considering my feeling because subconsciously there was fear that I wouldn't like what I found. Then there's the conditioning side of things. I was taught how to be a good man. And good men keep grinding.

The problem with rise and grind is that eventually there's nothing left to grind. If we struggle, strive, and fight for our life ultimately there isn't much of us left to live. I was a self-made man. Successful at making it look like I had it all together on the outside, but in actuality I was a broken soul, empty on the inside, and failing my family. If I was willing to be honest, my life was full of destruction. I had partnered with the accuser and believed all the lies.

A self-made man is one whom has learned how to be self sufficient and fought hard to become the man he wanted to be. He has struggled without the support of others to build himself. The self-made man earns his place by blood sweat and tears. This man is always striving even once successful.

One day he will look in the mirror many years from the beginning of that struggle only to have left a wake of wounded people in his path. The disconnection from his family almost complete, he is unsure of his own passions and dreams. That man has created a life motivated by fear. The fear of not measuring up, not having what it takes, and not being respected. Whatever the underlying struggle may be, the self-made man has a measure of success in some areas of his life at the expense of the others.

THE SELF-MADE MAN

STRUGGLE ALONE

Every man is taught that respect is earned, not given. I believed that when things were difficult, it was my job to shoulder the burden and crack on. I didn't need a handout or want help. I was going to prove that I had the right stuff.

How many men are dying all alone in their conquest to support their family and do the right thing? I don't believe that the average man is so full of pride that he's not willing to ask for help. In fact, it may even be the desire to do what is right that causes us to suffer alone. We tend to struggle all alone because we're trying to be the man that we're supposed to be and earn respect.

Our family only sees the successes, and we hide the failures. A business deal goes wrong; quick put another one together that works out better. God made us so strong and capable that we can fight all alone for decades, quietly dying a little every day.

I have many friends that feel they can't talk with their wives about business because "she doesn't understand." The truth is that if we keep them out of all the details of our life away from the home then when something comes up that we could use their help on, they don't have enough information or history to help.

Who do we depend on to learn how to be a good dad? Every once in a while we'll post a question in a private facebook group for Dad's and get 100 different suggestions that we ignore anyway. We are all alone in our parenting. I do it my way, and she does it her way. I had conversations about how we should parent, but in the end, it's one more private struggle.

I was dying on an island by myself of my design. I would pull myself up by my own bootstraps and get back to grinding. It was my duty and honor to bear the burden for my family so that they will be shielded from the stresses of life.

ALWAYS STRIVING

A man that is working hard is proof that there are good men. It's what a woman wants, a hard working man. We need to fight for success to show how it's supposed to get done. Lies, all lies.

Successful men have found both life flow and balance. I used to believe peace and flow happens after financial freedom. Once I crack the code and hit it big, then I can relax and enjoy my life. Until then, keep grinding. "God helps those who help themselves; right?" "Struggle by the sweat of my brow and all that."

Everything feels like a struggle; work hard, play hard, marriage is hard, parenting is a sacrifice, give until it hurts, and pray hard. Pick an area of life where someone else is more successful than us, and it's easy to see someone who is working hard. Life is not supposed to be difficult, but we believe that it is.

I would tell myself that One day I will overcome the struggle. However, until I become super successful, it's going to be a grind. The hustle was draining my energy and stealing my health.

Living In Survival Mode

I was living in a constant state of fight or flight, and I didn't even know it. Every month was a struggle financially which put me in survival mode. I was continually panicking about how we were going to make it. Even when in a successful season, the hustle continued. Fear drove me. The fear of losing momentum, or having to start over keeps us in survival mode.

Fear is what causes our brains to go into fight or flight mode. More accurately, it is fear that causes our subconscious patterns to rule the decision-making process. The unconscious patterns are what continue to create self-sabotaging behaviors.

I didn't even realize how much fear I agreed with: fear of missing out, fear of failure, fear of success, fear of losing momentum, fear of having to start over, fear of being discovered as a fraud, fear of losing my family, fear of ruining my kids, fear of divorce, fear of sin, fear of not having what it takes. This list is not even an all-inclusive; many fears rule us.

With fear mastering me, why was I surprised that the solutions I utilized for family struggles were either yelling at the family or running away to get some peace? Chasing leads for my business like a starving wolf or hiding from the boss is the same thing. I had created my life to be a constant struggle.

CORRECTION

Not being open to correction almost destroyed my whole life. I thought that I was open, and was good at having philosophical conversations, but Nissa was afraid of letting me know that my behavior was ruining the family. I don't even want to think about how my stubbornness was costing me spiritually. What's crazy is that I believed I was easily correctable. The truth was that I was very teachable, but my belief about, personality and things that were important hindered my ability to change.

How I behaved, is how I was always going to be. I could modify the obvious bad stuff, but I believed that my personality was not changeable. I was like the disciple Peter; open mouth, insert foot.

Self-made men are not open to correction. People, in general, do what they think is right. Other opinions generally don't land well unless it's very close to our own. If what we're doing is working, then why change? The problem is that often we don't even know the destruction that is happening in the wake of our actions. Most men who suffered through a divorce found out that they had a marriage problem on the day she kicked him to the curb.

POWERLESS

What's coming out of the mouth is representative of what's in the heart. The self-made man makes statements that don't allow him to be in charge of his actions. "I wouldn't have to yell if you would listen." "It's not personal; it's just business." "I can't lose weight because I travel too much." Blame shifting and giving other people the power over our actions.

It's like being a power vampire. We build ourselves up by stepping over the bodies of the ones that we believe were holding us back. Like a self-charging battery, we need to disempower those around us to keep going.

Thinking about some of the things I would say is quite sobering. "Be quiet; I can't think!" "Leave me alone; I need to relax." "I'm getting out of here; I need to recharge." Most interactions felt somewhat innocuous but the result of years of pushing people away and pushing them down created a world full of powerless people around me.

It's the exact opposite of how God is with us. God empowers us through grace, freedom, and love. He gives us every opportunity to be successful even at the cost of allowing mistakes. As a self made man, it was never ok to mess up around me. "Why can't you just do it right?" I would say. My older kids still have some of the lingering effects of my powerless behavior. In the end, it's those who are terrified which are controlling.

I was killing myself emotionally, and all I wanted to do was become the man that God called me to be. I wanted to do things right and be an amazing father with an incredible marriage living in the flow of financial blessing while being spiritually abundant. But, how? It felt out of reach.

MY GREAT AWAKENING

I felt trapped by my life. Most people feel the same way at some point, but that didn't make me feel any better. It's getting to the other side of the breaking point that can be dangerous and often causes people to blow up their current life. I believe that one hundred percent of the time it only takes some Godly truth and little life tweaking to take our lives from striving to thriving.

At that moment, however, I felt trapped, and it was easy to blame those around me. I never came out and said that my kids were driving me nuts, but my behavior did the talking for me. I didn't directly blame Nissa for my feelings of inadequacy, but I treated her like she was doing something to me. It felt like I was dying a little every day.

Family and friends were making me miserable. More powerless talk and blame shifting. I felt trapped by the ministry and had to show up every Sunday until the day I die because a good man never goes back on his word. I blamed work for not allowing any free time or earning enough money. Where I was living was too expensive, the neighbor's dog won't shut up, and I can't get a minute of peace in my own home, can't everyone leave me alone!

After a long day of work, I just wanted to be left alone. At the end of the week was more of the same. Please give me some space so I can breathe on my day off since Sunday is church day, I only get the one day. Hide, disconnect, and struggle with all the people who need so much of me. There wasn't much left to give.

I even started to blame God. He was making it hard for me so I will learn how to be a good Christian. He was teaching me how to be tough and take it like a man. All the great men of God that I knew had gone through crazy stuff. "Never trust a man without a limp," I was told on several different occasions by several different great leaders. The enemy has fed us, men, some giant lies, and it has perpetuated through the generations as wisdom. One of those is the lie that I am not good enough. At that moment at the café, I believed the lie.

I don't have what it takes. I'm not a good man. I'm not a good husband and father. I will never be successful. I was leading worship every Sunday, and no one knows that I'm depressed. My children want a hero, and my wife wants a knight in shining armor, but I am a failure. I am no champion, and I'm dying inside.

THE CHASM

I dropped the bomb on my wife over the phone. "Hi honey, I'm calling because while sitting here I've realized that I'm not happy." The words felt like a thousand pounds. I could hear her heart freeze on the other end of the phone. "It's not you or the kids, and I can't seem to put my finger on it, but I'm not happy. Can you pray for me?" What I didn't realize at the time was that I had just jumped across a giant chasm full of shame and guilt. Floating towards the bottom, like a leaf in autumn, was my man card. Darn thing must have fallen out of my pocket during the leap.

It was difficult for me to admit to my wife that something was wrong. Mostly it feels like I should have it all together. I mean, I'm a man right! Men are strong and bold. We're champions! If not now, then soon because we will keep fighting until we win or die.

Weeks went by as I wrestled with the survival of my soul. Every noise at home ground me down a bit more. It didn't matter if it was laughing or crying, everything felt like a direct attack. What I didn't know at the time is that I was already on the journey to peace, joy, and freedom, just because I was willing. That giant chasm of shame and guilt that I mentioned earlier is what keeps men trapped. We feel stuck because we can't cross over to the life that we want until we're willing to fall face first into a steaming pile of dung, figuratively speaking.

I'm not even sure why telling Nissa that I felt horrible was scary. Maybe she would leave me, or we would have to go to counseling. Doing so, however, was the first step towards living full of joy, love, life & power.

After what felt like an eternity which was in reality only a few weeks, the day finally came. The answer descended on me like the dove when Jesus got baptized. I had just finished yelling at everyone for making me late to church, then He spoke. "Ryan, joy comes from the inside, not the outside." God had just reached out to me in my darkest moment; when I felt utterly alone and worthless. "Duh!" I thought while driving my family to church. "Joy comes from the inside." I am responsible for creating an internal environment where happiness can thrive.

In a swirl of emotion from, shame to honor, from love to fear, I felt alive for the first time in years. The words, "joy comes from the inside" echoed through my head all service. I think I lead worship that day, but honestly, I don't remember much. Joy comes from inside of me. What does that even mean? How do I fill up with peace and happiness when everyone wants so much from me? From that day forward I went about discovering what it means to be responsible for creating an internal environment of joy.

I wrote a book about this journey called *FUNDAMENTAL: The Transforming Power of Having Fun*, so if you're interested in that specific journey, then you'll enjoy that book. But for our purposes here, I'll skip ahead in the story to the part where I got my man card back.

"Then the Lord God said, 'It is not good for the man to be alone; I will make him a helper suitable for him.'"

Gen. 2:18

The honor of every Lancelot is a Guinevere, and mine happens to be named Nissa. She loves me fearlessly. She is not responsible for my happiness, but cheers for and supports me. When I've been knocked down, she nurses me back to health. Nissa is my sounding board and my confidant. I lean on her when I feel overwhelmed, and our life together is that of fearless lovers.

Don't go telling the wife, "See honey, you're supposed to support me!" It is for me to take ownership of my soul's wellbeing. It's my job to make sure that I feel good enough, strong enough, smart enough. It's her honor to love me through the journey. Sometimes, it means staying quiet while I work out the details. Other times, she needs to push my buttons, so I'll realize that I believe a lie.

It wasn't a quick journey to this place where she loves fearlessly. It took many years of getting past my junk and learning how to live in the truth. That was only on my side, and then she had to deal with her stuff. The pathway to becoming Godmade is not straight. Fortunately, God makes our paths straight, so as we begin to work out the details, he points us in the right direction to a thriving life.

GETTING THE STORY RIGHT

It is written on our hearts to become the man we were created to be. Men long to win, conquer, discover, adventure, and be respected for it. Respect from others, especially our family, is essential; however, unless we respect ourselves, it won't matter how much support comes from others. Often our mind is the ultimate battlefield. God doesn't shame, accuse, or belittle; that's the job of the accuser.

Lost in a world of guilt over my inability to pay the bills consistently, I believed that I didn't have what it took. My decision to spend time with my family instead of putting in extra hours is what kept us broke. More blame, shame, and failure.

Facts on their own don't have meaning; we ascribe meaning to them. Truth trumps circumstances, feelings, and the past. If my wife is running around crazy doing things, and not paying much attention to me, that is a fact. Whether it means she doesn't want me, or she would rather spend time with the kids, or whatever story I'm believing is up to me. The truth is that she loves me and is probably feeling overwhelmed by trying to be everything to everyone. She would ask me for help but knows that I want to be left alone after work, so she's playing the good wife. The story that we believe will dictate our response, so it's important to keep the story straight.

Paul writes in the love chapter, Cor. 13:6-7 "Love takes no pleasure in evil but rejoices in the truth. It bears all things, believes all things, hopes all things, endures all things." The story that we should believe is the best of things. The truth is that God believes that we have what it takes. He is on our side and is rooting for us.

"Finally, brethren, whatever is true, whatever is honorable, whatever is right, whatever is pure, whatever is lovely, whatever is of good repute, if there is any excellence and if anything worthy of praise, dwell on these things." - Phil. 4:8

It's not hard to get to a place of believing that things are going against us. The stuff we go through creates a worldview by which we end up seeing other's actions. Often the skeptic feels that people are generally liars because they have been lied to and taught to lie. Those who struggle with giving or receiving love got there by being broken many times. It's our struggles that provide the story that becomes our reality.

I believed the lie that I needed to do more to be more; I had to choose to be there for my kids or provide a good living for my family. I was taught that we have to choose one or the other.

The truth is, many men are present with their families and also work hard and provide well. I don't have to choose between family or fortune. It's on me to awaken to God's truth.

The scripture, "You cannot serve both God and money." Matthew 6:24; is referring to which one is our master, not that we must choose between God and money. Our choice is to allow God to be our provider instead of the god of money.

I had believed that it was righteous for me to choose to be with my family and suffer through financial difficulty or to sacrifice my health and desires. I was trying to be a good Christian man. In the striving to do things right, I missed out on the blessing of allowing God to give me all things according to his Word.

I am a Godmade man.

CHAPTER 3

FATHER OF FATHERS

THEREFORE, IMITATE GOD LIKE
BELOVED CHILDREN.

EPHESIANS 5:1

I used to live like a boy trying to win approval from a harsh father. Reading my bible out of obligation and trying to be good most of the time, I struggled with earning His approval. Many times I've heard from the pulpit, "God tests us so he knows he can trust us." Wow, Really? The God of the universe, the maker of everything, Mr. All Knowing, all-powerful, omnipresent has to find out if he can trust me? I can tell you this, a father knows his children.

One thing I can count on is how my children will behave. I know them. I don't need to set up little tests to find out if they will honor, respect, and obey me. If even, I can trust my kids to be themselves, and still give them the freedom to mess up, then we can rest assured that Father God knows us.

> "God created man in His own image, in the image of God He created him; male and female He created them. ... 31 God saw all that He had made, and behold, it was very good."
> GEN 1: 27,31

I am not a result of broken DNA but rather a product of design. It is essential to believe at my very core that God made me the way I am because He thinks it is right.

Pain, however, has a way of forcing us to make decisions about what is truth and what isn't. Years before I met my wife, I was heartbroken by a failed relationship. It crushed me at the time, and I fell into a deep depression. I didn't eat, couldn't sleep and had real trouble differentiating truth from pain. I took my pain to Jesus.

It wasn't too long before He showed me His love and told me about the woman I would eventually marry. But during that time, I learned how to seek him despite the pain.

Father God led me to Ecclesiastes 9:7; "Go then, eat your bread in happiness and drink your wine with a cheerful heart; for God has already approved your works." I was shocked by the statement that Solomon writes, "…God has already approved your works." How could God approve of what I do, if I don't even approve of my actions? Then it hit me, the problem was that I genuinely believed that God's approval was based on behavior.

God sees us as He created us, not how we created us. Even though there are many times that I fall short, His love for me is never changing. He knows me, the real me. The one whose heart is pure, loving, kind, honest and free. The person that I saw in the mirror was the screwup that was good at causing pain, being selfish, and was a slave to, "getting it right or get punished."

I had a picture of Father God based on how I was raised, church leaders, movies and television, and any other father figure in my life growing up. I saw a God that sends people to hell for messing up and punishes them for failing to be perfect. This was my base of understanding. It's a natural conclusion for anyone, but the truth of God, the Father of Fathers, is much different than that. He has plans for me to prosper and not to harm, for a future and a hope (Jer. 29:11). If I know how to care for my children and give them grace for messing up then how much more my Father in heaven knows how to treat me.

Heaven isn't a reward for good behavior, it's the destiny of every Christian. I am saved and set free not by my behavior and how good I am, but by the blood of the Lamb. Likewise, we also cannot fight, run, or hide from God's love. It is eternal and unconditional. He's a good, good father.

KEEPING IT REAL

The difference between a lie and truth is often very subtle, and the intention isn't always malice. Most of the time leaders are trying their best to help keep us guys in line. Unfortunately, the message can come across opposed to the truth. Getting it right requires grace, mercy, and the freedom to really mess things up.

It becomes easy to agree with a lie because of our experiences. Growing up in a home where the father was an authoritarian, it would be easy to believe that God is the big bearded boss in the sky. Our misconceptions about the character of God impacts both how we read the scriptures and our identity in Him.

We are sons of the Father of Fathers, and inside of that sonship, we receive identity about who we are and what liberties we have. It's easy to use what we gained from our earthly fathers to apply in extreme measures to Father God. However, God is love.

> **Lie:** Men need to work hard to be in a relationship with God.
>
> **Truth:** God's yoke is easy, and his burden is light. (Matthew 11:28-30)

I attend churches that are non-denominational and quote things like, "It's a relationship, not a religion." Even in the freedom of those places, I still felt ashamed of my behavior outside the four walls of the church. Can I honestly be real with the people I fellowship with on a regular basis?

Men's groups are notorious for perpetuating the lies of the enemy. What happens when you get a bunch of men in a room with an inconsistent understanding of God. Someone will say, "we pray at 5 am because prayer is supposed to be a sacrifice." Rock-pile prayer, I've heard it called. Yeah, that's about what it feels like. Being on the chain-gang knocking on rocks until they turn to gravel. But our relationship with God is not supposed to feel like an impossible struggle.

The intention is to help guide each other into better behavior. Typically the leader has had a breakthrough in that area, wether it is porn addiction, alcohol, drugs, or something more like a prayer meeting. The leader sets the tone for the group, so if the one in charge doesn't have an accurate picture of the Father of Lights then it's no wonder that we end up with a belief that being a "good man" is difficult and requires a lot of discipline.

The truth is that God really likes us. He is on our side, and wants to see us flourishing in the fullness of who he created us to be. He wouldn't have sent Jesus to liberate us from the, law of works based salvation, only to make things difficult. He is love. That makes Him kind, caring, and supportive. He is willing to go through whatever struggle we have without judgment and will walk through fire for us.

God takes the burden of every challenge we have so He can walk through it with us. Picture two bulls yoked together plowing a field. One of them is powerful and has done this countless times before. The other is young and learning to be powerful. They are placed together not because the powerful one needs help plowing but so the young one can learn how to do it and discover his strength.

I'm referring to God as the Father of Fathers because it is his design for us to be great fathers. Some men don't get to have their own child, but that doesn't remove the destiny of being a father. There have been other great men who fathered my children well, like their youth pastor Seth and one of my close friends Liviu.

These men poured into their lives and taught them things that my perspective couldn't have.

We are also designed to be great leaders. Why else would we be yoked to the Leader of Leaders? Keep in mind that every place of lack for us isn't actually a place of lack because We are yoked to God and He lacks nothing. The strength of God in our weaknesses makes us powerful. That young bull may struggle for a bit in the beginning, but when they move forward together, he will begin to see himself like the big, powerful, peaceful, and unchainable beast that he was born to be. It's in the co-laboring where we learn our identity.

> **Lie:** I can have approval or freedom, but I can't have both.
>
> **Truth:** Love creates freedom and I am approved as a son of The King of Kings. (Gal 5:1, Ecc. 9:7)

The struggle for approval is usually a daddy wound that get's applied to God's character. The default parenting style of most is either authoritarian or "do whatever you want." It takes some intentionality to learn how to parent powerfully from an authoritative perspective. Authoritarianism is favoring or enforcing strict obedience to authority, especially that of the leader, at the expense of personal freedom.

The opposite parenting style of this is to let kids flourish in freedom at the expense of learning healthy boundaries, honor, and value. The consensus amongst researchers is that the authoritative approach yields the best adults. The difference is that an authority figure has proper guidelines that are designed to protect but also allows the freedom of personal exploration with the understanding that a mess might get made.

God is a great representation of the authoritative approach. "Follow these guidelines so your life goes well and you flourish in the fullness of everything I've given you." The freedom we have is complete freedom. Because of Jesus, we no longer need to struggle with eternal insecurity. As Paul writes, sin is a product of the law and apart from the law there is no sin. Misbehaviors then are no longer leading to hell, but cause us to stray from the path of abundance.

As you'll likely read a few times in this book, Ecclesiastes 9:7 says "Go then, eat your bread in happiness and drink your wine with a cheerful heart; for God has already approved your works." This verse has become my hearts fall back place. Whenever I start to feel the lack of approval I'm reminded that God has already approved of me. Our actions do not create real identity for us, but rather a chosen identity. I surf, therefore, I'm a surfer. If I stopped surfing, I would no longer be a surfer. I cannot stop being a son of God. He sees me just as I was created. There is nothing I can do to separate from His love.

Whenever I allow my earthly experience to impact my eternal perspective it will always lead to an earthly version of God. Even good experiences can lead us astray. This is why it is of utmost importance to be grounded in the truth of God's word and be so connected to God that we know Him beyond experiential distractions.

GOD'S SON

God is waiting for us to step into the fullness of our identity as sons so we can stand as men. Grace and mercy are not the freedom to continue sinning, they are the freedom from the punishment for sin. Jesus died for ALL of our sins before we were ever born. He covered the ones that I committed before I received salvation and the sins that will be committed many years from now. All sins are covered by the blood of Jesus.

Punishment actually keeps people stuck in sin and doesn't prevent improper behaviors. We must eliminate our eternal insecurity right now to begin to experience the fullness of God's freedom. In Galatians 5:1 it is written, "It was for freedom that Christ set us free; therefore keep standing firm and do not be subject again to a yoke of slavery." The bible tells us not to go back to being partners with the devil's plan for us.

Every time we agree with the accuser about our salvation we are now trapped by sin. Freedom from pornography came for me once I realized that getting snagged by the porn monster wasn't going to send me to hell. It's freedom (love) that set me free, not the yoke of religion. Love never brings fear and I was afraid of punishment. Love's perfection actually drives the fear of punishment far from our hearts. 1John 4:18

The beauty of grace is that it allows us to deal with the root of sin. Punishment only deals with the action but doesn't help support freedom from the cause. Once we are free from punishment, then we are empowered to break free from the repetitive negative behaviors and actions that keep us stuck.

This kind of fearless love isn't taught much in church. When I was a pastor I had a real fear that if I caused someone to stumble, then their salvation was at risk. And worse, I might have a millstone tied around my neck and be tossed into the sea. Could I really lose my salvation because I inadvertently led someone astray by preaching freedom? It is a real fear that a pastor has for "his flock" that something he might say could cause someone to fail in their relationship with Jesus. None of us want to be the source of someone else's misunderstanding. However, the scripture in Matthew 18:6, "but whoever causes one of these little ones who believe in Me to stumble, it would be better for him to have a heavy millstone hung around his neck, and to be drowned in the depth of the sea;" is talking about passing down an offense, not causing someone to sin.

Even writing this, I know someone might take it wrong and use what I'm saying to stay stuck in their lifestyle. The thing is, getting free is best done by giving an example of freedom and how to properly handle that liberty. Will I go to hell if I do wrong, no? Will it potentially affect my relationship with my wife and kids, yes. Because we have moved from the law of sin and death to one of liberty and love, there will be a line that we must learn how not to cross. "It is the glory of God to conceal a matter, But the glory of kings is to search out a matter." Prov. 25:2. God makes our journey to righteousness semi-mysterious because it's the only way for it to stick.

I love coaching soccer, especially the littles. Six-year-olds think they know it all, and I'm successful with them because I've learned the secret to getting them to do what they're supposed to do. I lay out all the clues as to what is the right thing to do is, until they come up with the answer themselves. Similar to the Socratic method of asking questions to lead someone to a solution, God allows us to earn our knowledge of how to behave well without punishment. Embrace freedom and long for righteousness, then the rest will take care of itself.

I am approved by God.

WHAT IS HOLY SPIRIT SAYING ABOUT ME AS A SON?

CHAPTER 4

JESUS IS OUR EXAMPLE

LOVE EACH OTHER JUST AS MUCH
AS I HAVE LOVED YOU.
JOHN 13:34

My father is a wise man, full of understanding. Whenever working on something like this book, I make sure to chat with him about it. He taught me that we never really get the full picture, so stay humble in the estimation of your knowledge. Even though I was feeling a lot of the Holy Spirit's empowerment to write this book, I went to him with some questions. The questions were unimportant compared to his response which was, "It's simple, just love like Jesus."

No truth could be more important in our journey to becoming the man that God intended us to be than to love like Jesus. The bible is full of flawed characters like King David who was a man after God's own heart but stole another man's wife, got her pregnant then had him murdered. Peter, is another example of a manly man passionately following Jesus but denied Jesus when it mattered. Abraham, the father of faith and nations, couldn't even walk in his identity without fear and almost lost his wife because of it. In Genesis chapter twenty, Abraham tells the King Negev that his wife was his sister because he was afraid that they would kill him and take his wife as their own. We have many men to encourage us and exhort us to do well in The Good Book, but only Jesus is the complete example.

Jesus is entirely God and entirely a man. It's likely that I will never completely understand what that means, but it gives me hope none the less. There is a picture of Jesus running around in my head that looks a lot softer than me. "Suffer the little children to come unto me," He said. I didn't feel like I could ever measure up to Jesus' example. I was too rough to ever be like Jesus. At least, I used to be that way until I realized one thing. Jesus led Peter, the sons of thunder, and a host of other ruffians. None of those men would follow a weak leader.

Jesus wasn't soft, he was patient and kind, and long-suffering like the fruits of the spirit tell us, but he wasn't a pushover. It's like writing something on social media, and then it gets interpreted wrong in several different ways? Yeah, that's how it works when reading the Bible without complete understanding. The early church tried to force people into holiness by rules and religion. They controlled the Holy Scriptures, and only a member of the clergy was allowed to interpret them. They grew in corruption and power until, despite their initial efforts to bring salvation to the world through a specific methodology, they failed to represent Jesus well.

They painted him, sickly and meek. They wanted people to be calm and powerless, so they depicted his suffering that way. I've been to the Louvre and seen these paintings up close. They are designed to create an emotion and belief in a weak and suffering servant.v It's the paintings of the fishermen though that caught my attention. These simple men of action and humble lifestyles followed a man that they believed would be their salvation.

The reason they followed Jesus is the same reason we follow him. He is very good at loving us through our shortcomings and encouraging us to live in freedom. He turned over the money changers tables and made a whip to force the charlatans out of the temple not out of anger, but out of love. He did it to protect his people who were being sold lies about His Father. Jesus endured torture for hours at the hands of the Romans and was still expected to carry his cross miles to Golgotha. Even after all the torture they expected him to last longer on the cross because clearly he was a strong man of strong will. Regardless of the picture I had about

Jesus one thing was clear, He loved fearlessly.

FEARLESS LOVE

My wife taught me, fearless love. She may not have been fearless while doing so, but how she represented her love for me felt that way. It's a freedom to be who we think is right while discovering the better way. It's not free of correction or input. It feels a bit like this, "Even though you're treating me bad right now I still love you and believe the best of you." I learned later that she was afraid to share her needs with me, but there is still space in this kind of love for her to be empowered to speak her mind.

Loving is part of our calling as men. We were made for love, to give it and receive it. Since Jesus is the perfect picture, then we can follow his example. A woman accused of harlotry was brought to Jesus so they could test him. By law the people had the right to stone her to death. The first thing he does is to stoop down and say nothing. Our only account is that he wrote on the ground. Maybe it was the sins of those standing around. Perhaps it was a scripture of God's mercy. Or maybe he just doodled on the ground some picture of him fishing with his friends.

What happens next is a perfect picture of fearless love. He stands up and says, "He who is without sin among you, let him be the first to throw a stone." Then he goes back to playing in the dirt. He doesn't move, doesn't get out of the way of hurling rocks. He is defending her without any fear of reprisal. That's what he's earned by having a perfect response. He heard them, then showed her the love of the Father. He didn't see a sinner that he needed to rescue, instead saw a daughter of the King of Kings, and he gave a response that would eliminate the accuser.

Jesus didn't stand in front to protect her from the rocks with his own body; he simply showed them what it means to love those the way that the Father does, and it set her free. One by one they dropped their rocks and left. 'Straightening up, Jesus said to her, "Woman, where are they? Did no one condemn you?"' She said, "No one, Lord." And Jesus said, "I do not condemn you, either. Go. From now on sin no more."

Notice there were no guidelines for her to follow. No multistep programs or accountability groups. He didn't try to plug her into any system to keep her from falling again. As Peter reminds us, "Above all, love each other deeply because love covers over a multitude of sins."

Fearless love allows people the freedom to be themselves despite potential mistakes.

FALSE FREEDOM

"I will LET you be free until there is a mistake, then I will clean up your mess. I will show up as a leader for you until you can be trusted again. Eventually, if you keep making mistakes I'll need to have you take a step back until you can figure out what's going on."

-Said, Many Leaders With Their Behavior

False freedom gives permission to those we are leading to do things their way as long as it lands at our end point. It's controlling and manipulative and doesn't allow for the power of those in our lives to show up. This is what I call *fear-based leadership*.

Fear-based leadership can take many forms, from the dictator to the happy go lucky, to the silent type. At the end of the day, does the leader require that we land at a specific point or is it ok to have a different result than expected?

Jesus was a fearless leader. Picture Jesus sleeping in a boat that is in the middle of a very rough storm. It's rough enough to make seasoned sailors fear for their life. Yet, Jesus remained at peace. Why? There are two reasons as it pertains to leadership. First, he was teaching them that, peace, is the appropriate response when things seem crazy.

The other reason he was asleep is that he was letting them lead. He was leading the disciples to their own greatness through LOVE. Freedom is the ultimate expression of love. It says I love you regardless of the outcome. Jesus was willing to see the ship sink if that's all the people he left in charge were able to do. But, he knew them.

He knew that they were amazing sailors and in the natural, they had what it takes to make it through the storm. He also knew that they were powerful men in the kingdom of God and they needed the opportunity to be successful.

Matthew 8:26 - "He said to them, "Why are you afraid, you men of little faith?"

This scripture is mostly interpreted through the eyes of our fear-based leadership examples. Do we believe that Jesus was making fun of them? Perhaps he was calling them names? Maybe he was pruning them by pointing out their failures? This is not God's way, and it's not Jesus' way either. He was not upset with them at all.

Jesus was exhorting them to greatness. It could be written this way, "Why are you mustard seed men afraid." Let me show you how to deal with an impossible situation. First, remain at peace, then assert your authority as sons of God. I know you have what it takes because I've seen you heal the sick and do the stuff. You are amazing men with the faith that it takes to move mountains. I trust you.

This is what I call LOVE based leadership. When a mistake is made the proper position is first, peace, then love. Perfect love casts out all fear. If the person we are leading believes that we love them above punishment then they know that the next thing out of our mouth will be helpful.

For example a love based leader would says something like this, "You were free to run with that project and it didn't land where I thought it would. What do you think is the next step from here? I trust that your plan will work out because I know who you are and the power that you carry. Don't be afraid, be at peace. Trust that the wisdom of God has been planted in your heart and move forward with my love."

A truly supported person can then ask for help without fear of being found out that they don't know the answer. In that process, those who have a different vision than the leader will go their own path and move on. The ones who have a similar vision will come alongside and flourish.

True freedom creates a space for success. Whereas false freedom only creates a space for compliance. If God is the ultimate representative of a leader and Jesus is our earthly example, then it's time to start building leaders who are familiar with freedom and the power that it brings.

I love fearlessly
as Jesus does.

"I'm no longer willing to be a leader that only has compliants about people around me. I want powerful leaders who are creating other powerful leaders. I am willing to love people through the journey regardless of the outcome."

- The Godmade Leader

CHAPTER 5

GOD IS THE LIST

But seek first the kingdom of God and his righteousness, and all these things will be added to you.
Matthew 6:33

I'm about to share one of the most significant shifts in my life. When I started to implement this, everything began to change for the better.

If the average churchgoer made a list for how to prioritize life, the standard answer would be God, Family, Work, Ministry, then Self. The answers may vary, but for the most part, it would be God first and Family second. If we look at how they live it's more like: Work, Ministry, Family, Self, then God.

Actions dictate which things in our life are a priority. No matter how hard we try to get things straight, in the end, something will suffer from a lack of attention. Most people want to put God first on their list; then life gets in the way. Here's the problem, if we make one a priority over another it's communicating something about our love. If I tell my kids that God is more important to me than them, then it shouldn't be any surprise that they might grow up resenting God. If I put my kids before my wife, she might understand, but when the kids leave, we will have a relationship based on kids that are no longer there.

What I discovered about prioritizing life has led to abundance in every way. Instead of putting God at the top of my list, now God is my list. He is the foundation for everything that I hold in my life to be important. The implementation of this has lead to a stronger connection with God, my wife and I have been like newlyweds ever since, work has felt almost effortless at times, and the kids are happy and doing well in school.

God is my relationship with my wife and kids. He is my business, and when I'm surfing, playing soccer, or running a triathlon, we are doing it together. There is room for Him in every area of my life because he is my life. God isn't separate from my life and my life isn't separate from Him. God is the Alpha and the Omega, the first and the last, the beginning and the end. He is the morning and evening star, and he knows and loves me beyond words.

Take for example spending fifteen minutes with God every morning uninterrupted in our prayer closet; this is a good thing. But, then the toddler wakes up because he's peed the bed. Do I let my wife deal with it so I get my God time? "Not now, I'm spending time with God, go find your mom." However the situation goes, life will always get in the way. Is fifteen minutes enough time to have a good relationship with God anyway? How about thirty minutes or even an hour?

The point is that we have an everyday life to deal with, which makes being alone with anyone a real challenge; including our wife. We set up a date night, and nothing gets in the way of date night! Unless someone is sick, or something important happens at work, or church is holding a special meeting. Even if we try to protect that one day out of seven to spend with our wife, it's not enough anyway. She deserves way more attention.

Thinking about priorities is a bit like building a house. Is the roof more important than the walls? Is a door or window more important than the foundation? All those things are needed to have a complete, secure house. So really none are more important than the others. While building a house though, if there isn't a solid foundation and it's not a priority, then the rest of the house will suffer. Each step along the way impacts how the rest of the house functions, and if we want to live in a house with no fear of it crashing down on our head, then at each phase along the way there must be a priority.

We are building a life, a family, and a legacy. Each function of our life should be working in harmony with the rest. There is a spiritual order to things which makes life work well. God is the foundation, my wife and I are the house, marriage is the roof, and the kids are what make it a home. Work, ministry and other external stuff that we do is a part of our legacy, and life fulfillment so it should not be shunned, but it also should not be prioritized above the things that are most important.

I was fat, out of shape, mentally drained, overworked, felt under appreciated, and dying inside. That does not sound like a good leader and is even less like a good foundation to build a family on. Remember, God is in every part of the list, and each piece of the life puzzle should have Him at the center.

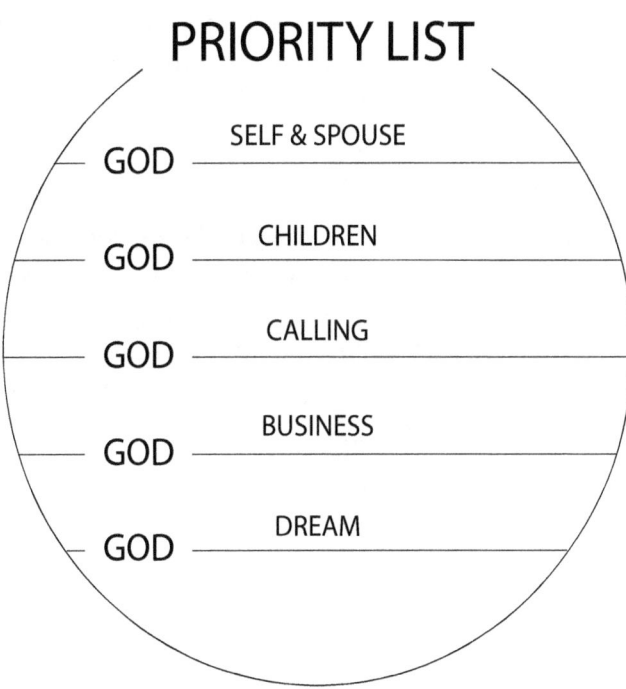

ME & SHE

When on a commercial flight, the attendant will give the rundown of what to do in case of a "water landing." Oxygen masks will fall from the panels above you. Put one on yourself first, then your child. The adult is the priority over the child because, if the caretaker is unconscious then how is the kid going to carry that person out of the plane to safety? In taking care of the child before the adult, it would put both of their lives in danger by not prioritizing the adult's safety first.

Nissa and I are one, just as Christ and the church are one. As two animals are yoked together to plow a field so are we as leaders of our family. If either of our health, well-being, and spirituality suffer, so will our ability to lead the family.

As the leaders of our family, it is of utmost importance that we are fit to lead. If I end up in the hospital with a stroke because I spent the last 20 years ignoring my health and wellbeing then how is that going to help my family? If Nissa pours everything into the kids and me, trying to be the "good wife" and her health and wellbeing suffer for it, then she will not be fit to help lead.

By the time our kids are in college, there's not much energy left for spending time together traveling the world and doing fun things. We've sacrificed every part of who we are so our kids can do great things. But, what a horrible example to leave behind. They will do what we did and be good moms and dads and drain themselves to nothing in the name of "good" but not God.

Samuel said, "Has the Lord as much delight in burnt offerings and sacrifices as in obeying the voice of the Lord? Behold, to obey is better than sacrifice, and to heed than the fat of rams." 1 Sam 15:22

Sacrificing for our children and wife is good. Better is to be obedient to the call of the Lord. He has called us to serve our families, not sacrifice for them. Jesus already laid down his life for us, so we get to become the man he created us to be.

I am not suggesting that we become selfish, self-absorbed men with a, "me first" attitude. Jesus is our example, and he laid down his life for us so that we can be free. What I'm suggesting is that we stop sacrificing our health, emotional well-being, and spiritual needs to be a "good man." When a leader sacrifices too much, they are only going to crash and burn.

Hangin' with da boys every night is not part of preparing to be a good leader, but exercising regularly is. If I'm feeling stressed out and need to get away, then I'm free to take a day to myself to recharge. My daily actions have built a connection with family, and they won't mind if I have some me time. If I want to exercise, often I'll do it when I'm not needed, early in the morning or late in the evening. It doesn't have to be a time sacrifice to exercise; it's better than watching Sports Center. I used to play soccer or basketball during my lunch break and eat quickly on the way back to the office. In the new priority list, we're not putting ourselves first but instead loving ourselves well.

Our spiritual well-being is essential to leading our family. God is in every part of the priority list so when I'm taking time to exercise; I'm also spending time with him. Two hours of surfing means one hour of praying; because it's hard to pray while shredding a wave. When I go to play soccer, I'm praying on my way there and while warming up. I make it a priority to have God in everything I'm doing. I could be swimming, and we're having a good time hanging out. I still have prayer closet time, read His word and soak in worship, but making God a part of my overall wellbeing has revolutionized my life.

MARRIAGE IS A COVENANT

Salvation and Marriage are the only covenant relationships in my life. Our kids did not get to choose us. My relationship with them means the world to me, but they didn't say, "I do." They have a personal life journey of which I am not in charge. They get to love me my whole life, and I am an irreplaceable role in theirs but they too will have a covenant relationship one day, and it won't be with me.

A covenant is like a contract but not really. In a contract, we agree that one party pays a certain amount and the other party does a service in exchange. A contract is an even exchange of value. A covenant is where two people say they will do something regardless if the other person keeps good to their side of the deal. If we had a covenant deal for me to wash your car in exchange for ten dollars. That deal means that you would pay me ten dollars whether I washed your car or not. It also dictates that I would clean your car whether you paid me or not.

In a marriage, I promised to love, honor, cherish, and she promised the same. We formed a covenant relationship with God and our families as witnesses. I don't get out of that deal if she doesn't keep up her end of the bargain. I told my wife that I would do anything for her, and be by her side through thick and thin. I gave her my heart and said, "you are free to do what you want with this." I am willing to be wounded and mistreated because I want to be by her side forever. I was 23 years old, what did I know about life? I didn't realize the weight of that commitment. We have been married a long time now, and it has only been in the last several years that I've understood what that vow means.

Our relationship deserves my utmost attention. In the same way that I need to be sure that I'm healthy physically, our relationship is a part of my overall wellbeing. I won't sacrifice time with my wife to spend alone because it is good for my soul to be in a healthy marriage. My marriage and relationship with the kids are part of taking care of myself.

Nissa and I don't have a date night set up. We hang out every night. Occasionally I need to travel for work, but for the most part, we are together often. Four little kids don't make it easy to get a babysitter anyway, so we put the kids down early enough for us to spend time together. Having a date doesn't mean we need to have a romantic overpriced low-quality meal. It's all about connection, and we must have time to connect.

Making our marriage relationship a priority over the kids has made everyone happier. When we are in connection, they seem to behave better. If the kids start acting up and begin misbehaving, then I know it's time to be alone with Nissa.

As the leaders of our family, our kids are looking at us and learning how to be married. Our sons are learning how to treat their wives, and our daughters are learning how they should be treated. In the end, we are not responsible for how they handle marriage, but we're also not innocent. How we behave toward each other will impact our kid's marriage either for better or for worse.

THE KIDS

After, self-care and marriage, the kids must take priority over work, ministry, and everything else that we deem important. There is an unfortunate epidemic of kids being ignored and treated as second-class citizens. They get pushed around and told that they don't matter by our actions. Even though it was my dream to be a dad, I was guilty of communicating that I didn't want the kids around. It came from spending too much time in survival mode. I was trying to get through another day without losing it, so being needed was added strain.

Money was tight, and I was the sole breadwinner. If I didn't come home with cash, then we didn't eat. Sometimes Nissa had to leave a full shopping cart at the grocery store and come home because the bank card wouldn't work at checkout. Talk about humiliating; this is the same place she shops at every week. Then there is the call, "Hey, are we out of money? I tried to go shopping but had to leave the cart at the checkout." My heart sank out of my chest as I scrambled to come up with a date when we could get some groceries.

Naturally, I spent more time hustling to make sales and get my family fed. But in doing so, and not having my priorities straight, my health suffered, my marriage suffered, and my kids suffered. I was doing this for them, but my communication was, "leave me alone so I can work." Or, "leave me alone so I can rest from a long day of work." Even though in my mind I wanted to prioritize the kids, in reality, I was putting them last on the list.

Now, when I need to hustle, we're a team. I ran a 70.3 Ironman race a few years back. Training for that was brutal and took a ton of time. I did my best to keep the time running, biking, and swimming to hours while the kids were asleep or at school, but that was not always possible. I made sure everyone was on board with the extra time it was going to take. I let them know that there was an end in sight and I would be back. Most importantly I kept my priorities straight. God was in the journey, I would connect with my wife about what He was sharing with me, and I got rad downloads for the kids.

The balance was there. We were all happy even if the time was slanted toward "me time" for a little bit, we were all connected and in the journey together. Once the race was over, things swung the other way for a bit. Honestly, my body was so beat up from 3 months of grueling training and an even more challenging race, it was nice to spend time playing with the kids and hanging out as a family. Along with the "awakening" came a love for connection, so I longed for a connection to family.

It is well and good to want to keep things in the proper order but a whole separate challenge to walk it out. Even after having worked so hard to get everything straight, my behavior sometimes doesn't communicate what I want inside. There is a constant shifting as life comes which causes the need to pause and reflect on how things are going. It's helpful to have a wife that feels she has the freedom to tell me when I'm not getting it right. If I self-reflect honestly, then I know when I'm not getting it right, and her help in seeing it is more of a confirmation.

Pride is one of the killers for prioritizing life how I want it to go. I might think, "I've been a little off lately. I'll right the ship and move on." But, it doesn't work that way. When the priorities get out of alignment, then people get hurt. It might be small hurts, but if covered over with time, they can grow into painful memories that feel impossible to rectify. When the wounds are fresh and open, that is the best time for making things right.

My kids never turn away when I come to apologize for ignoring them. Nissa feels very loved when I openly seek her heart. When I'm feeling out of sorts health-wise, it's a lot easier to get back in order sooner rather than later. It's never too late to start getting things right, and it's never too early either. Cleaning up the mess that I've made is never fun, but is always rewarding.

God is involved in every part of my life.

CHAPTER 6

TRUE LIES

IT'S THE WAY YOU LIVE, NOT THE
WAY YOU TALK, THAT COUNTS.
JAMES 3:13-16 (MSG)

We are men of action, and our actions speak the truth. If I say that I love my wife but then talk to her like she's stupid, then my actions call me a liar. If I desire to be with my kids, but when they ask me to play with them I say, "just a minute" but never get around to it, then my actions are communicating the truth. If actions and desires do not line up, then it's time to change.

Paul writes of his struggles with this, *"For what I am doing, I do not understand; for I am not practicing what I would like to do, but I am doing the very thing I hate." - Rom. 7:15.* Remembering that Paul was not Jesus, we can be encouraged a bit. We all struggle with being double-minded, especially when it comes to our behavior. Our intentions are good, but ultimately our actions speak the loudest.

Behavior can be categorized in one of two ways, it's either an act of love or a cry for love. Most behavior is not an act of malice, but rather a cry to be seen, heard, or valued. Even when people are intentionally evil, they are still attempting self-love. Hate is never the motivation because hate is an inappropriate act of self-love.

Here are some examples of how behaviors don't line up with intentions. If I yell to my kids to stay out of the street, it's an act of love if I'm trying to keep them safe from cars. If however, they keep ignoring my warnings and there is no immediate safety issue at hand, it could be me saying, "please respect my authority."

Another example is when someone flips me off on the freeway.

They feel slighted in some way, and want to communicate their need to receive respect from me. When my wife is nagging me to fix the fence, it is a call for me to show her love and honor her need to feel safe and that her opinion is valued.

God created us to be inherently good. The fall in the garden of Eden didn't change our nature but instead gave us an understanding of how to be manipulative and deceitful. Love is still our nature and our motivation. Most of my struggles have come from believing that self-love was the safest path to peace, power, and freedom. Typically when we have an incorrect core belief, it came from when we were young. The truth is that God's love, vulnerable connection with those in my life, and the freedom to fail without eternal consequence are the safest path to peace, power, and freedom.

I could blame my parents or circumstances, but it doesn't change the reality that my story needs to change. A core belief in psychological terms cannot be deleted and must be superseded by a superior view. What makes a belief superior has to do with its effect on my life. Reinforcing the story I want to believe is an excellent first step. For me, "Self-love is inferior to "Godly love." I have that one on repeat for whenever I'm feeling low on love. My wife has had a core belief that she is only valuable when serving. Her new story is, "I am loved and valued because I exist and my actions won't change that." There are lots of stories that get stuck in our mind usually around eight years old. "I never win anything." "I'm a failure." "Having expensive things proves that I'm worthy." "Success requires sacrifice."

Here's some good news, *"With God nothing will be impossible." (Luke 1:37)* This scripture is why I named my second son Luke. There is nothing impossible for God. Whatever the struggles we are having as men, husbands, or fathers the solution is close at hand. We are not climbing Mt. Everest to find the answer, we only need to cross the river to the promised land.

There are three emotions that every man needs to feel fulfilled.

We must have power, peace, and freedom. All of our actions surround our desire for these three feelings. Joy and happiness are found inside of peace. Freedom to be ourselves, have adventures and discover what we are capable of are a must. Finally, we long for respect, a desire to be wanted, and the power to lead.

It's time to stop believing the lies, and start living in the fullness of God's calling for us as men. I am good enough. I do have what it takes. My family wants me. I am acceptable just the way I am. People see me for who I am, they want to hear what I have to say, and I matter. I don't need to manipulate the world, my kids or my wife into loving me.

The truth is that we have needs. Sex is not as much a physical need as it is an emotional one. I believe in marriage; sex fulfills all three of our core emotional needs. The main reason men are more available to open up after sex is that their emotional needs have just been met. It is our need to feel: powerful, freedom, and peace, which is the key to unlocking our relationships. If we come home from work and have a sense of peace, we are free to be ourselves, and we feel respected as the leader of our home, then being open emotionally is easy. The emotions are what we need most, and our family is not responsible for providing them.

Children are always a good example for adults because their emotions are just amplified versions of our own. If a child is angry, sad, hungry, happy, or scared, we know it. Adults are trained to keep their emotions inside and appear to be at peace even when they are screaming inside. The parents who get the most compliments are the ones with children who are peaceful, happy, and self-sufficient. For lack of a better term, "good kids" are not needy.

As men, we are in a similar situation. The ones who aren't emotionally needy are the ones we call "good men." I want to be a "good man" as much as the next guy, but needing to be seen as a good man is the opposite of what garners that kind of respect. The man who demands respect is the one who is not well respected.

Struggling for freedom will cause people to hold on tighter, and often to get peace we need to be very loud, so everyone knows to be silent. Getting those feelings from an external source is the lie, and filling them up internally is the truth.

PEACE

Peace is an inside job, and although a measure of it can be achieved through outside influences, it's still an inner work. Making a big sale can bring peace for the moment. We go home and feel like everything is going to be ok. Then the bills start coming for the next month, and the peace is gone again. That's the effect of outside influences on our peace.

Our wives and children can do the same thing. All the kids are behaving well, Nissa is happy and feeling loved, there is peace. Then Micah hits Luke in the eye with a ninja sword, and now there's screaming. Nissa forgets that Glory needs to have a costume ready for school tomorrow and dinner is half finished. Just like that, all the peace is gone.

When we've learned how to allow God to be our center of peace and fill up the inner peace cup, then it's easier to deal with these kinds of situations. We need to get the peace that passes all understanding in our daily life, not just on Sunday after worship.

Joy and happiness live inside of peace, so one of the ways that I keep my center is by being joyful. It's a choice and a practice to be full of joy. While stepping out of depression during my great awakening, I learned how to overflow with joy from the inside. I wrote a book about it, "Fundamental: The Transforming Power of Having Fun" if you're interested in finding out more about that journey. The key is not in finding things that you enjoy, but rather enjoying the things that you already have in your life. I don't enjoy my kids screaming, but I do enjoy my kids. I've learned how to allow them to be kids and still honor my own need not to have my ears bleed.

I'm not saying it's easy to be filled with peace, but I am saying that it's simple. Seek the Prince of Peace, believe His truth about who we are and eliminate the lies. We need to feel peace, so seek to be full on the inside.

FREEDOM

Wild, adventurous, dangerous, dreamers wanted. We long for freedom like a wave longs for the shore. It's part of the reason we play and watch sports. And why we go bounding into the forest to burn wood and meat. Men need freedom in as many forms as we can get it. Women do as well, which is why they are attracted to us while we are wild and free.

Society, culture and our grandparents tell us that we need to settle down and lock-in. "Men need to grind hard and be steadfast." Even though those sentiments have some value while learning how to stay connected to family, they are also freedom killers. Our only escape becomes watching sports because we are not afforded the time to pursue them ourselves. We are supposed to go to work, then come home and eat together as a family. Then we can put the kids to bed and spend time with the wife. By the time all that ends, we are tired and ready to get up early the next day and do it again. The weekend is our salvation from a life of bondage.

On the weekend though, it's time to mow the lawn, complete they honey-dos and be emotionally connected to the kid's activities. Some dads take it to the extreme and push their kids to be successful in sports, and take their lack of freedom out on the 14-year-old referees and other parents. Sunday is church day, so all that's left is 3.5 hours on the weekend to sit and watch football, basketball, baseball, or whatever sport we can find. Summer is like torture. The kids are out of school, and everyone is free except for me! Oh, and there are no sports to watch!

Our need for freedom drives a lot of our behaviors. Honestly, most of us feel trapped by our lives. There is no freedom to be the man that we dreamed of being. We don't even know what we would change if given that freedom. Then the midlife crisis hits, and we buy a motorcycle to steal back our weekends. Ahhhh, the open road. We are wild again. We can breathe again.

Many families are ruined by one or both spouses seeking freedom. The crazy thing is that "freedom" is best found in a fearless, loving relationship.

Once I discovered my joy and learned that connection is what I needed even when disconnection is what I wanted, then I was free to be myself. I pushed away everyone in my life so I could be alone and have a moment to breathe but that only created a bigger trap.

Freedom comes from being fulfilled personally. The only way to feel free to be ourselves is to find fulfillment with our families, work, finances, and health. Galations 5:1 tells us, *it was for freedom that we were set free.* Freedom is so important that the "great commission" didn't come with rules, just a mandate. "Go into all the world (This is Freedom) preaching the gospel to all creation (This is Dangerous)" Mark 16:15.

The key to feeling free to be ourselves is to fill our hearts. God made us to give love and receive love freely. Godmade men feel free.

POWER

I saved this one for last because it's the least understood or talked about need. While thinking about some scriptures that bring a tremendous feeling of purpose and power I've found that I don't even know their full meaning; but, they stir me up. *"From the days of John the Baptist until now the kingdom of heaven suffers violence, and violent men take it by force." - Matt. 11:12.* What does that even mean? I've heard many great men of God teach on this scripture, and still, I don't understand the fullness, but it's provocative, and it stirs me up!

Here's another one, *1 Cor. 4:20 "For the kingdom of God does not consist in words but in power."* Now I feel stirred up! There are about 250 scriptures about various forms of power and many others that make us feel courageous and strong. The kind of power I'm referring to is the emotional need to be empowered for greatness, love fearlessly, and lead with confidence.

Power is respect. It is liberty to lead and be followed with admiration. Power is about being loved and having others receive our love. Power is a core need for everyone, and it can manifest itself in incorrect forms.

Society has taught us to flex our strengths, and have contests of strength and wit. Supremacy is fought over power in leadership roles in every aspect of life. We demand respect by being loud, or strong, or angry. Fear is often the weapon of choice while fighting for power. And, it is a call for love.

The desire to be respected, honored, and admired is believed to be proof that we are loved. Therein is the core of one of humanity's most profound lies, that we are not acceptable as we are. The truth is that God loves us, respects us, honors us, and is proud of who we are. There is nothing we can do to earn his love and nothing we can do to lose his love.

Identity is the key to feeling powerful beyond measure. I am the son of the King of Kings, joint seated in the heavens and earth, a royal priesthood a holy people. I am loved, and God, who holds the universe in the span of his hand, knew me before the beginning of time. The all-knowing, all-powerful, omnipresent creator of all, loves who he created me to be. He sent his only begotten son to die in my stead so I can be in a relationship with Him. His promises for me are yes, and amen and His mercies are new every morning. I am approved, valued and set free.

I stand firm in the knowledge of who I am and whose I am. Whenever I'm feeling helpless or hopeless, reminding myself of my identity is a great help. Past prophetic words and scriptures of his promises are powerful for raising countenance. It is my journey to greatness that is responsible for feeling powerful. It's when I begin to put that burden on those around me that I start to slip back into using anger and my physical strength to feel powerful. Who I am in Him is my power.

> My actions align
> with my intentions.

What are my actions saying that I don't want them to say? What should I change?

CHAPTER 7
WINNING HER HEART

GO ALL OUT IN YOUR LOVE
FOR YOUR WIVES, EXACTLY AS
CHRIST DID FOR THE CHURCH.
EPHESIANS 5:25-28 (MSG)

I've been in some potentially life-threatening situations. I almost drowned once or twice. I fell backward off of a rock while free climbing in the desert. And, I was in a motorcycle accident on the freeway. None of those were as scary as the moment that I heard this from my wife. "Ryan, this isn't working for me. I don't know what needs to happen, but I can't keep going like this." That was the moment I felt closest to death.

There are two great joys in a man's life which are incomparable to any other conquest, experience or accomplishment. The day she says "I do," and the day our child is born. I remember when Zeke was born I felt like everything I had done to that point was meaningless. It was the same with all my kids. On the day of their birth, I was beyond expression. They captivated my heart as only a child can.

Everything was about to go away. It took ten years of marriage to really screw things up, but it only took one day to make it right. Ok, that's a bit of a misnomer because it's not just one day of work to fix ten years of being an ass. It is, however, a daily effort that makes for an amazing relationship.

If you ask most men, we think our relationship is good, and if you ask most women, they would privately say no. One of the reasons is that it is easy for men to put their heads down and keep moving forward. We have a singular focus, and like a mule, we can keep going until we die. Women are equally as tough, but they secretly die every time we treat them like one of the guys.

With our friends, we can talk to them like they are idiots. We can fight, call them names and make fun of each other. Women don't treat each other that way. Making fun of one another's outfits could mean they never speak again. For guys, cracking on each other is par for the course.

Our wives, however, deserve an honor that no one else on the planet gets. Because she is my best friend, there is grace for our differences but to love, honor, and cherish means something significant.

I didn't think I was that bad. I loved my wife with all my heart. I would die for her and the kids. There's nothing I wouldn't do for her! At least, that's what was in my heart, but it is not what my actions communicated.

> *The sink is full of dishes again* — "I just got home from work, she can do it. I mean, she's been home all day with the kids doing nothing."
>
> *The laundry basket is overflowing* — "She never does my clothes. It's always the kids' clothes or sheets. I can sleep on dirty sheets, but I need a clean shirt."
>
> *Baby needs a diaper change, and it's terrible* — "pretend like you're on an important phone call."
>
> *She got lost* — "What are you stupid? I gave you directions like nine times."

I would never actually say any of this to her, nor do I truly mean any of those thoughts, but my actions did all the talking for me. After years of selfish actions, there were volumes of horrible non-verbal things said.

After a long day of work, I want to sit down and not be needed. I need to be left alone, so I bark at everyone until they give me space. And then they do provide me with space. Our families will leave us alone until one day they feel like they would be better off without us. And then we have what we wanted; we're all alone.

Except, it's not what we wanted. We wanted to be loved, respected, honored. We wanted someone to hold, love, and to be her champion. We needed to have a purpose beyond working and find some measure of peace. We wanted to be "the man"!

The truth is, that while seeking to be left alone, I communicated that I wanted disconnection. I said, "give me space, I can't breathe." I was dying for freedom, peace, and power. What I needed was a connection.

ONE SMALL THING

It was a typical day. I had come home from working in Waikiki and had sat in horrible traffic for longer than usual. It was later than, so everyone had already eaten, and the sink was full of dishes. My kids were happily playing out back, and my wife was bathing Luke. I stood in the living room with everything I ever wanted, to be left alone, and that is what I felt, alone. We have a picture on our refrigerator from our wedding day, and it reminded me of how much I loved this woman. I remember looking at the stack of dishes and thinking, "The last thing I want to do right now is dishes." Then I thought about how she probably doesn't want to do them either. If I truly loved this woman then why would I make her do it?

Sure, I had a long day at work and sat in miserable rush hour traffic, but I love this woman. I don't want to watch my wife scrub the kitchen clean before she can relax so I can have 10 minutes of downtime. I made a decision that day that I would do at least one thing every day to communicate that I love her.

Then my kids came in, jumping around me. Daddy's home! Yay, daddy's home! They squealed with delight. "They are excited to see me. Why do I keep pushing them away? They are only this young once. They will only be this excited to see me at the end of the day now, while they're little." So I sat on the floor, and we played. Ten minutes later they were off in a whirlwind to play something else.

That was it. Twenty minutes of my life spent showing my wife and kids that I love them and now I am free to do what I want. She didn't even say anything about the kitchen, nor did I. Not until the next day when I was getting ready to leave for work, "Oh, by the way, I didn't get a chance to thank you last night for cleaning the kitchen for me. It was the last thing that I wanted to do, and when I came out and saw that you had cleaned it, I felt very loved."

Wow, one small act of selflessness communicated love. I began to call before my lunch break. "Is there anything I can do for you while I'm in the city?" On my way home while stuck in traffic, "Can I stop at the store and get anything on the way?" Thinking of her needs has become my way of doing things, and what it did for our marriage was priceless. But that is only one small piece.

THE RUDDER OF A SHIP

This chapter began with my story of Nissa telling me that she wasn't willing to put up with the way things are going anymore. That story happened three or four years after my great awakening. I was helpful, and for the most part, I learned how to be happy and stop yelling. I was good with the kids, and I did lots of little things that communicated my love to her, but she wasn't happy.

There are two pieces to this story, but for now, we'll talk about my tongue. I was bad at this. It's much better these days because we have a deal that Nissa can tell me when I'm talking to her like a jerk. But, she still puts up with more of it than she deserves.

I hear some of my friends talk to their wives and think, "Dang dude, you're lucky she puts up with you." It's probably the reason why most marriages fail. We forgot the most important part. She deserves the same respect and honor that we want.

Simple passing comments spoken in a condemning way are incredibly hurtful. It's not all our fault, people can take things however they want but if we record ourselves talking to the wife with other people around then played it back we might be embarrassed. Lord knows she is embarrassed and hurt.

I never yell at my wife, in fact, we may not have ever been in a fight. Certainly not the way we've heard some other people go at it. Even still, my small words, comments, and attitudes create a wall of pain that keeps her in a perpetual state of misery. It's not all my fault; it never is one-sided in a relationship. It takes two to make a relationship, and it takes two to break one. But, my little digs and her lack of speaking up created what seemed like an insurmountable obstacle. She was no longer ok with our relationship the way it was going.

GUINEVERE NEEDED A CHAMPION

My wife needed a champion to rescue her from the fire-breathing dragon. I was the dragon, and my fire burned her and the kids on a small but continual basis. I was doing so good compared to the past, but there was more than just my own life in need of saving. I had to make things work for all of us. It was time to slay the dragon and win her heart.

How I speak to her, not actively participating in the daily duties, and not being humble were all breathing fire on my relationship. They burned my wife and my kids regularly. No more! I actively seek to slay the beasts that destroy relationships.

The problems were not all on me. Nissa had her stuff to deal with and work through. And like I learned from various marriage groups and classes, she didn't want me to fix anything, just listen; so that's what I did. I listened to her talk about the problems she was having, and I tried to hear my parts without saying anything. We had a moment of impasse where the only option was to forgive everything on both sides, and start over or call it quits.

Calling it quits was never an option. We truly loved each other, but it was time to make some changes. We had four kids who needed us to get it together. So we did the impossible and completely forgave. For her, that meant she would overcome her childhood trust issues, and I would be wide open for correction. Just like she had rescued me with her fearless love, it was my turn to return the favor.

This next season was about learning how to win her heart back. I had to become her champion and stand in the gap for our marriage. It was time to take my lumps and fight my old behaviors and selfishness to allow her room to heal. It was time to help her become who God created her to be.

I speak with kindness and love.

How will I win her heart today?

CHAPTER 8
MEN OF ACTION

LET US NOT LOVE WITH WORDS
OR SPEECH BUT WITH ACTIONS
AND IN TRUTH.
1 JOHN 3:18

Marriage is holy and is a sanctified picture of Jesus (the bride) and the church (us). It is not a free pass for having sex without sinning, nor is it an automatic porn removal tool. As a pastor, I've fielded some strange and extremely common questions about marriage. Inside of a loving, God-centered marriage, is a prophetic picture of Christ and the church.

Most of us probably had this scripture read at our weddings, *"Husbands, love your wives, as Christ loved the church and gave himself up for her..." Ephesians 5:25*. It feels like an impossible call for us men to treat our wives like Jesus. Just the thought of having to be like Jesus makes my head shake in wonder. Yet, it's not that big of a stretch if we think about the example. Jesus simply covers our sins with love to create an eternal connection.

Our kids should be able to look at our marriage and see the salvation message. In the past, most of the time they would see a picture of what it looks like to be on my own. They would see connection as a struggle, and Jesus as someone who loves in spirit, but not in works. They might have grown up believing that Christ is a symbol and not a person, and it wouldn't be a stretch to think they might have gone astray.

Marriage is about creating a constant connection through action. *"Love is patient, love is kind and is not jealous; love does not brag and is not arrogant, does not act unbecomingly; it does not seek its own, is not provoked, does not take into account a wrong suffered, does not rejoice in unrighteousness, but rejoices with the truth; bears all things, believes all things, hopes all things, endures all things." 1 Cor. 13:5-7.* Every one of these are actions.

LOVE IN ACTION

Patience is not the art of skillfully looking like nothing is wrong when the man inside is stomping around like a child. Real patience is, having so much compassion for what another is going through that our peace remains even during stressful circumstances. Lack of patience comes from the lack of perceived love.

Love is kind. Being kind gets represented a lot of times as becoming the "nice guy." Genuine kindness is loving someone regardless of their actions. That does not mean I will stand there nicely while being spat on. I am allowed to love myself. Using action instead of reaction enable the space to get our behaviors straight. Reactions are those knee-jerk responses that cause us to swear, fight, run, or yell and can come across unkind. Pausing for a couple of seconds allows us to chose kindness and manage our actions. Choosing to be kind is one of the great acts of love.

Jealousy does not communicate love but is a behavior rooted in fear and insecurity. Psychologically it's connected to imposter syndrome, which is a label for, "If she finds out who I really am then she won't want me." Jealousy doesn't make the other person feel wanted but instead communicates a lack of trust in the very person in whom you are trying to trust. Love is pouring grace on fears.

Love doesn't brag and is not arrogant. By definition, arrogance is having an exaggerated sense of one's own importance. Yeah, I've done that. I can't even count the number of times I've thought about how much I do for the family, and how little help I get. Those feelings come from a lack of peace, feeling disrespected, or even feeling trapped. In a Godmade relationship both people feel like equal parts. Love doesn't need validation by supporting its own importance.

Being inappropriate is one of my favorite past times, but Nissa tells me how embarrassed she feels when I **act unbecomingly** in certain situations. Love decides to tone it down. An unbecoming behavior in a loving relationship is pretty much any action that embarrasses the other person. I'm not suggesting that we become boring and proper. If however, the goal is to communicate love and my wife is embarrassed by an action, then "love" will change the behavior. At the very least, talking about it openly, allows her to feel loved.

Fortunately, love **keeps no records of wrongs** because I would have a lot of making up to do. Keeping no record of wrongs is one of my favorite aspects of unconditional love. Keeping track of how often we get disrespected, dishonored, and treated poorly is like filling a water balloon with syrup. If we don't stop that behavior, it will pop and make a huge mess. I tell Nissa when she did something that hurt me because I don't want it to build up and fester. Let it go, or talk about it then let it go, those are the only options in a loving relationship.

Two wrongs don't make a right. True love **doesn't celebrate when the other person messes up** as bad as we did. There is no even score to keep. Love celebrates truth because that is where freedom is. It has been said that, misery loves company, but what we need is someone who can be strong with us. If love isn't keeping track of wrongs, then it also doesn't need to cheer on a mistake.

True love, "...**bears all things, believes all things, hopes all things, endures all things.**" We are to champion each other to greatness. I support her through thick and thin, I believe in her, and I believe her. We hope together and fight together and grow together. Love conquers all.

Love looks like action, and our actions speak louder than our words. It's what we do on a daily basis that is our mouthpiece. Words are important, but nonverbal communication shouts the loudest.

Actions that don't seem loving are rooted in the need for love. When we get angry at someone for cutting us off in traffic, it is an act of crying out to be seen and respected. When we yell at our kids to get out of the street, it is an attempt to show love. We are saying, "what you're doing is dangerous, and I need to communicate to you quickly that I don't want to lose you to ignorance." Rest assured that every action whether inappropriate or not is trying to show love or receive love. When we allow fear to be the leader, then the action comes out wrong. Love pours grace on fears.

> 1 Peter 3:7: "In the same way, you husbands must give honor to your wives. Treat your wife with understanding as you live together. She may be weaker than you are, but she is your equal partner in God's gift of new life. Treat her as you should so your prayers will not be hindered."

RENEWED RESOLVE

It was time to put all this love into daily works. I started with the dishes, but it grew into much more. She didn't just need someone to help around the house, although she did need that help. Nissa needed me to talk to her better and be softer with the kids. It was time to get honest with what I wanted and what it would take to get it.

I want to have the most amazing marriage imaginable. I want to help my kids feel confident and self-sufficient. I want to have time to pursue an active lifestyle and to travel with my family. It's important to me that I have the freedom to help others have the same loving relationships, happy family, and spiritual connection that I have.

Those are some lofty goals, but I know that it's possible. God created man and woman to be together as partners in life. He created us to be in communion with him like friends hanging out. Like Luke 1:37 says, "With God all things are possible."

Winning her heart begins by putting love into actions. When I see the basket of laundry sitting on the couch, I know that she wants them folded. I also know that she didn't have time to fold them herself or they wouldn't still be sitting there. Love takes a step forward, and the laundry gets folded and put away. It's funny because, in the beginning, I had no idea where any of the clothes even went. I couldn't even tell the difference between the clothing sizes. I kept asking things like, "Is this Micah's or Lukes?"

Taking internal inventory of how I feel helps to figure out how Nissa feels. Women can be so mysterious, they say one thing and mean another; or they do something to help us come up with the right answer on our own. Men say what we mean, and do what's on our mind. I never used to think about what was going on inside.

Now, I'm asking questions about why I yelled at the kids. And what I need to help get that internal peace that I'm after. Taking a moment to think through what's going on inside helps me to be the man that I say I want to be. I began to see how I was treating my wife and kids and started learning if my actions were working for them. Having an open heart to feel my own pain and needs has been my key to becoming what I call a Godmade man.

Our actions and desires must be in alignment with each other. Past hurts can hinder that from happening. I take them to God, clean up whatever mess I made with people, and then get honest about what I need to do.

THE ACTIONS THAT MATTER

Every action matters. If we want to be the man that God called us to be, then we must take responsibility for our actions. How are we treating the ones that we love? How do we treat our co-workers? How do we behave when no one is looking?

We must be true to our design. Ask the question, "Who do I want to be?" I decided that I wanted to be the guy that everyone wanted to be. It's a lofty goal, but I decided that I wanted a marriage that was off the charts amazing. I want my kids to think, "My dad was the best dad ever, and I want to be just like him when I grow up." I wanted a life that made me come alive instead of steal life from me. I made it a priority to play more and be physically healthy.

My life today is by design. I took responsibility for where it was and how I was, then changed everything that wasn't working for me. It took several passes to get things right because I have five other people in my life who also want the life of their dreams.

Take a look at your life. All aspects of it are by your design. If we balme others for where we are then we play the victim. Blame gives power, so if you blame yourself, then you now have the power to change it. It's time to take massive action.

I prove my love with actions.

What do I need to change right now, tomorrow, and next year in order to have the life of my dreams?

CHAPTER 9
THE SECRET WEAPON

A HUSBAND HAS THE
RESPONSIBILITY OF MEETING THE
SEXUAL NEEDS OF HIS WIFE
1 CORINTHIANS 7:3 (TPT & NLT)

THE SECRET WEAPON

I'm not going to sugar coat this next section. This is a book for men, and we all know that there is one thing on our mind that doesn't make it into most Christian books. We've done all the touchy-feely stuff, and looked at our inner child; now it's time to break out the big guns. This next chapter is all about how to get some lovin' (for married men of course).

The average married American is only intimate once per week, and it's not uncommon for it to be less than once per month. The experts say that lack of intimacy doesn't necessarily mean there is a problem with the relationship, but it's certainly a big red flag. When we're first married it seems almost impossible to keep our hands off each other, so what causes the shift?

There are many reasons for the struggle for intimacy. Financial stress is a big one, the fear of getting pregnant is another (for women). When it's men who are the ones with the lack of desire, it can be from stress or the lack of feeling respected in a relationship. For women, it could be everything from the sink full of dishes, to the kid's school, to her own work stresses. I have found that even with all the things that could keep a couple from passion, in a loving connected relationship intimacy is never a problem.

Sex is the fruit of connection, so if there is no connection, then there will be no sex. The problem, however, is all in the mind. Men are good at compartmentalizing different parts of our life. We can be almost wholly focused on one task while completely forgetting about something else. Women, on the other hand, have all their thoughts in one big bowl. If my wife is disconnected when I'm trying to be with her, it can feel like she doesn't want me; which is not true.

The two big sex drive killers for men are disrespect and feeling unwanted. Since respect and being desired are what turn men on, if we don't get those things then we would rather not waste the energy. In a previous chapter, I talked about filling up our respect meter from the inside, but there is also a need for respect from others, especially our wife. Proverbs says this twice, *"It is better to live in a corner of the roof than in a house shared with a contentious woman."* It appears once in Proverbs, 21:9 then again in Proverbs 25:24.

How important is it to a man to live in a home with a woman who is full of peace? According to Solomon, it was a critical point to make. With a thousand wives and concubines, Solomon probably understood this better than most.

Truthfully it's the same for our family and how we treat them. If we're always barking orders, and trying to force them to behave a certain way, then it can be equally as painful to be in the house with us.

When my home is full of strife, I feel powerless. I'll tend to shut down emotionally and become very hard to please. I tend to push away the very people whom I desire to be with the most, and I become part of the problem.

Lack of peace in a home communicates to everyone that they aren't acceptable just as they are. It causes kids to seek approval, and husbands and wives to hide, fight, or run. It doesn't matter where the source of strife comes from, all that matters is how to get the peace back.

Connection is the key to unlocking a home full of peace, kids full of joy, and a marriage full of intimacy. Communication is one tool that most counselors suggest, but honestly, I was an excellent communicator even before I learned what matters most. Another connection tool is spending time together, but I spent a lot of time with my family even before our big breakthrough. Complete connection starts with us men.

Sometimes my wife will catch me doing the dishes and say, "You are so hot right now." I'll notice that the floors could use some sweeping and she'll walk by and give me a little "yeeowwzzza." Helping with the kids, taking on some of the tasks that she has planned for herself to complete and being on top of my own personal growth are major turn-ons for most women.

Here's the big secret to getting the wife fired up. When there are a lot of things on her mind, she can't be fully involved in the bedroom. And, she wants to be there with us. Women are not much different than we are in regards to their physical needs. They crave physical connection and, actually want sex as much as we do.

Women want to do it with the man that they fell in love with. The one who would sit and stare at them, and listen to everything on their mind — the man who would help throw rocks at their enemies and come to their rescue when in trouble.

Step number one to getting things back on track is connection. Reconnecting with the kids will prime the pump for everything else. Children are always ready to start over no matter how big of a punk we've been in the past.

Love is not really in question here. I've always loved my children, but my actions told them that they were not allowed to be children. I can blame that on my personal issues with feeling like I wasn't allowed to be a kid growing up. Those are my own lies. Those old stories though, tend to leak into adulthood and cause behavior that we don't want.

In Luke chapter eighteen Jesus is having a serious teaching meeting. People start sending their kids to go be touched by him.

The disciples begin rebuking everyone, trying to protect Jesus from the masses. But Jesus called for them, saying, "Permit the children to come to Me, and do not hinder them, for the kingdom of God belongs to such as these." The King James version says, " Suffer little children to come unto me…"

Kids are open and loud with their emotions, don't operate under the proper protocol, and believe that they have complete access to everything around them. Adults are trained to keep our feelings inside. We follow the status quo and have learned that we have limited access to things. The kingdom of God is open and free. The more we play with our kids, and treat them with the same respect that we expect them to have for us, the more we will connect with how God created us to be.

Connecting with our kids is step one, and connecting with our spouse is step two. Action, is the name of the game, no pun intended. As men, we're good at letting our actions speak for themselves, and with connection, it takes putting our love into actions.

It's sad, but studies have shown that 84% of women say they have sex to get their husbands to help with housework. Housework and other things that women have on their plate keep them from connecting. It's not just about intimacy; it's all forms of connection. Women will often feel disconnected from their kids as well when there is too much that they need to get done. I didn't step up and help because I had been working all day and was mentally exhausted. If being honest, I was coming up with cheap excuses for avoiding doing the dishes. I'm happier now that I help around the house, and with the kids.

Getting back to the newlywed phase takes more than doing the dishes and changing diapers. It's time to sit and listen. I was always a good listener, and it seemed like I didn't need help in that area, but the truth was that there were things that she didn't feel safe sharing with me. My behavior wasn't open to conversation. I had made it clear that I didn't want to talk about my actions because they were justified. I was mean because I was stressed, or whatever the excuse. Either way, when confronted about my actions, I would bark until we moved to a different subject.

Ultimately we want to be the best leader we possibly can be. A quality leadership course will cost anywhere from two thousand dollars to twenty thousand dollars and up. Corporations understand this and spend millions of dollars per year on creating quality leaders. God is also interested in having quality leaders. The world's version of a leader is one who leads from power. God's version is one who leads from love.

When my wife comes to me with a comment about my behavior, she knows now that I will listen and not get upset about it. It's my job to reinforce that she is safe to come to me with anything. Even if what we're talking about is uncomfortable to me, I want to make sure that she feels safe in bringing it up. I am not responsible for how she feels, that is on her, but I am accountable for my actions. Because I love her and want to show her that she is loved, I will audit my behaviors to make sure that what I'm doing isn't reinforcing the old story that her voice isn't valuable.

It's time to be men of action, and allow our nonverbal communication to line up with what is on our hearts. When the Bible asks men to "love their wives" it's talking mostly about behaviors, not emotions. All men love their wives, but it is the story in our mind that keeps us stuck in negative actions.

THE BIG O

Once a connection with the kids is working, the housework is being shared, and we are listening to her heart, then it's time to talk about the physical. I feel one of the most underrated aspects of marriage is the female orgasm. Oxytocin is a hormone that is released only during climax. Psychologically it's known as the cuddle hormone and is linked directly to creating a bond. Studies have shown that regular oxytocin reception increases a desire to be with the one who helped bring that release.

Like sleep, the more we get, the more we want. The more times she climaxes, the more she will want to be with me physically. It's not just important; it's a requirement to maintain a healthy relationship. And according to the apostle Paul, it's our duty as Christian men – *"A husband has the responsibility of meeting the sexual needs of his wife. 1 Corinthians 7:3"*

Many women feel used when it comes to sex. A Godly woman might feel more used than a woman of the world because they feel it's their duty to put out for their husbands. "The wife does not have authority over her own body, but the husband does; and likewise also the husband does not have authority over his own body, but the wife does." It's not just this scripture that adds to the feeling of being used, but it also doesn't help. In the church, women are trained to give sexually to their husbands as a form of Godly sacrifice. Every time we use them to get our rocks off it reinforces this belief.

This question has done wonders for our physical relationship. Have I captured her heart today? Just like how men have intimacy killers, so do women. One of the biggest ones is, do they feel like they matter. Is their voice important and is it being heard? Is she allowed to be the Proverbs 31 woman that she has been trained to admire?

Having fun inside the bedroom starts outside of it. A lot of women can't climax because they are feeling self-conscious about their bodies. It's not all our fault; they do it to themselves. Women are mean to each other when it comes to body shaming or how they dress. Taking the time to snuggle and have non-intimate touching is a great way to increase her ability to get there. Unless you're in a hurry to get the deed done, taking time to hold each other and be close is necessary.

The biggest thing for a woman, why she can't climax is because she has too much on her mind. If there are dishes, cleaning, and undone stuff, she can't compartmentalize and will have trouble being fully involved. Even though they want to switch it off, it's just complicated. When she's feeling overwhelmed, sometimes all she needs to hear is that it's ok, and we're in this together. Neither men or women want to feel alone, so talking about how you will help in the morning or after, or whatever communicates love. Then, you must do what you said you would, or next time it won't help.

Whatever the reason is, we should make her orgasm our priority in the bedroom. It's not just for fun. There is genuine value in making sure that both people are satisfied physically. It's not always possible with kids because they wake up and need a drink of water and for some reason are incapable of getting their own. Whenever we can take our time to make sure everyone is getting what they need, the better relationship we will have; physically, mentally and emotionally.

CONNECTION

At the fall, there was a blame game that happened; *Genesis 3:12 "The man said, 'The woman whom You gave to be with me, she gave me from the tree, and I ate.'"* Adam straight up thew her under the bus and blamed God for giving him a partner that he couldn't trust. Wow! I would have smacked him in the mouth for that comment. Had Adam stepped up and admitted his fault for not being the spiritual leader things might have gone differently. One thing for sure is that the serpents plan all along was division, disconnection, and separation from God.

When God made us, he said that it was not good for man to be alone. It is imperfect for us to be alone. The enemy is always trying to bring us apart. My secret weapon is connection. It's not all about sex, but it is all about intimacy. We are designed for connection, and to be with the woman of our dreams.

When I think about my desires to have a home full of peace, it leads me to create opportunities for everyone in it to be filled with joy. Happiness, joy, and peace all come through a complete connection. Anything that distracts from that focus should either only last a short time or be eliminated. This is my secret weapon for having six people in a house that are enjoying being with each other. The kids love to play and rarely fight with one another when they are feeling connected to me. My wife is happier and feels the freedom to pursue her passions when we are connected well, and both satisfied physically.

Jesus died for connection, that is how important it is. Freedom is found inside of connection. Freedom to be who we were created to be, freedom to love and be loved. Our mandate as men is to create an environment that mimics what Jesus did for the church. It's not about being perfect, just about fighting for connection.

Intimacy is a two-way street.

What are the main intimacy builders in my relationship?

CHAPTER 10

CHAMPION

LOVE BEARS ALL THINGS,
BELIEVES ALL THINGS, HOPES ALL
THINGS, ENDURES ALL THINGS.
1 CORINTHIANS 13:7

The pride of every man is his wife. I have come to beauty's rescue and fought for her love. As the champion of her heart I long to see her happy with a life full of peace and pleasure. I am her's, and she is mine.

Time passes, glory fades, and life takes over. Bills rule, and daily tasks steal our focus. The champion becomes the caretaker and passion becomes a chore. The man dies inside a little every day because he is no longer doing what he was made for. Man was created to champion those in his care. "Be fruitful and multiply, subdue the earth and rule over it…" was the mandate from the beginning of time. Our great call is to create a world that is working in harmony with the life that we see for ourselves and our family.

How do I champion her heart? What are the steps? What am I supposed to do? The questions are endless. How much help is too much? How much is too little? Am I supposed to only cheer or should I participate? After 16+ years of marriage, and trial and error, I have come to realize that every woman will need something slightly different from their champion, but the core of her needs are the same thing.

She wants to feel loved first. It sounds basic, but as I've written in previous chapters actions are the loudspeaker of love. The bible mentions explicitly in several places that men are supposed to love their wives. The heart of a woman needs to feel loved. For some that would be that they need to feel like they matter and are an important piece of our life. The big three are seen, heard, and valued. Every person really needs these, but for a woman, it communicates love.

Secondly, she wants to believe that she has the freedom to operate on behalf of the family without fear of reprimand. Again, for us guys, this doesn't sound like a big deal, but the church has told women that they are second in command. The Biblical truth is that we are one flesh and my command is her's and her command is mine. Kris Vallotton wrote a book called Fashioned to Reign where he goes in amazing Biblical detail about the disempowering scriptures of women in the church, and all the other nonsense that has been perpetuated by those who didn't know better. It's time for women to rise up and feel free to operate as an equal part of our marriage.

Lastly, she wants to believe that her success won't destroy the family. Many an insecure man has squashed the ambition of a powerful woman. I, personally, want to see my wife and children do great things. Nothing would bring me more honor, than for my wife to be celebrated for her works. The call of a Godmade husband is to champion our wives and children to greatness.

I mentioned before about the Proverbs 31 woman, and since this is not a common scripture taught in men's gatherings here it is:

A DESCRIPTION OF A WORTHY WOMAN
PROVERBS 31:10-31

10 An excellent wife, who can find?

For her worth is far above jewels.

11 The heart of her husband trusts in her,

And he will have no lack of gain.

12 She does him good and not evil

All the days of her life.

13 She looks for wool and flax

And works with her hands in delight.

14 She is like merchant ships;

She brings her food from afar.

15 She rises also while it is still night

And gives food to her household

And portions to her maidens.

16 She considers a field and buys it;

From her earnings she plants a vineyard.

17 She girds herself with strength

And makes her arms strong.

18 She senses that her gain is good;

Her lamp does not go out at night.

19 She stretches out her hands to the distaff,

And her hands grasp the spindle.

20 She extends her hand to the poor,

And she stretches out her hands to the needy.

21 She is not afraid of the snow for her household,

For all her household are clothed with scarlet.

22 She makes coverings for herself;

Her clothing is fine linen and purple.

23 Her husband is known in the gates,

When he sits among the elders of the land.

24 She makes linen garments and sells them,

And supplies belts to the tradesmen.
25 Strength and dignity are her clothing,
And she smiles at the future.
26 She opens her mouth in wisdom,
And the teaching of kindness is on her tongue.
27 She looks well to the ways of her household,
And does not eat the bread of idleness.
28 Her children rise up and bless her;
Her husband also, and he praises her, saying:
29 "Many daughters have done nobly,
But you excel them all."
30 Charm is deceitful and beauty is vain,
But a woman who fears the Lord, she shall be praised.
31 Give her the product of her hands,
And let her works praise her in the gates.

Firstly, this is a prophetic picture of the bride of Christ (the church) and how we honor him with our dealings. Secondly this as an example of a wondrous woman who has the utmost support of her husband. If we take the literal from this passage, we can read that a Godly woman is honoring to her husband simply by being great. It is a man's honor to champion his wife to follow her heart and to sow, reap, give, and operate in greatness.

Some men feel challenged by a woman who is doing great things; such is merely insecurity in their own value. Embrace the part of our heart that longs for a woman who brings us great honor. Becoming her greatest fan, support, and confidant is what we want.

I am continually encouraging my wife to try things. One of her superpowers is having babies. I know, that might sound strange, but she had four babies pain-free (her words, not mine) and has helped other women to have amazing births. It is my honor to champion her to train women, write books, and do what's in her heart to do. I have no fear that her success might overtake my own. I would rather her fulfill her destiny than to feel like I'm the big boss.

What a huge lie it is to believe that I'm the boss. First Peter 3:7 reads, "…show her honor as a fellow heir of the grace of life, so that your prayers will not be hindered." Treating our wives like a lesser part of the marriage pie is not as God intended things to be. According to Peter, it will actually hinder our prayers. It is God's honor when I do great things. Likewise, it's man's honor when his wife does great things.

When it comes to being charitable, my wife will give away everything we own. Sometimes she will sheepishly admit that she helped someone with groceries, or gave a bunch of money to some cause. I always try to support her in those decisions. It happens all the time because her spirit is so contrite that she can't help but have compassion on the broken. It has honestly not always been easy for me because we have not been in the most stable of circumstances, financially. One truth I learned from Heidi Baker is that in the Kingdom of God there is always enough. So I champion my wife's generosity as I'm learning to trust that He is my source.

It's not a mandate for men to be the champion, but it's for our benefit. Ever since we were pregnant with our first son, my wife has had the honor of not having to work outside the home. As time goes and the kids grow, she has had a calling to do more and fulfill her hearts desire. I choose to champion that call in her life.

A QUICK TRUST RANT

Proverbs 31:11 (Amplified Version) "The heart of her husband trusts in her [with secure confidence], and he will have no lack of gain." Not trusting our wives is a massive mistake for married men. We are Godmade men, and we *"believe all things (1 Cor. 13:7)."* If you're nervous about someone else, she might be around who could capture her attention then become the man of her dreams.

Jealousy is dishonoring, actually causes trust rebellion, and is very unattractive. It is controlling, manipulative, and is a tool of the enemy. Being jealous is opposed to love, and communicates that, "my fears are more important than you are." A man or woman who is jealous will tear their house to pieces.

I want my wife to be so awesome in every area that I have made it my mission to support her in everything she does, no matter what. So, at the end of our lives, we will look back and smile because she showed that Proverbs 31 woman how to do it right. These verses talk about all the amazing things that she can accomplish because her husband's heart has shown her that she is important, valuable, and she matters. He trusts her.

Trusting each other is not only good for helping your wife to feel loved, but it's also a requirement to have a healthy marriage. Love believes the best. If we do not believe the best in our spouse then we are not operating in love.

> I champion my family
> into their dreams.

How can I champion my spouse?

CHAPTER 11

THIS CHANGES EVERYTHING

When disconnection is desired, connection is what's needed.

There is one concept that has influenced every significant change in my life which is this; when disconnection is desired, connection is what's needed. The decision to remain connected when the heart is screaming to be left alone singlehandedly transformed my entire life. My wife and I started doing incredible, my financial picture improved significantly, my health skyrocketed, and my kids felt like a joy to be around consistently. This one concept literally changed everything.

Getting closer when it feels like more space is what's needed is a bit counterintuitive. It feels that way because our "fight or flight" mechanism is kicked into overdrive. Stress, fear, pain, anger, abandonment, lack of love, self-worth and a whole host of negative emotions can trigger the amygdala to decide if it's time to run, fight, or freeze. Unfortunately, the majority of our life cause these kinds of emotions. The solution to most negative feelings is love, and feelings of love only come through a connection.

It's easy to come home from a long day of work and want nothing more than some personal space. We shout at the kids either literally or figuratively to leave us alone until we get what we want; we are alone. After years of coming home from long days of work only to push away the ones we love, we no longer feel loved, wanted or respected. We have officially disconnected completely.

What a man really needs is peace, freedom, and a sense of power. The desire to disconnect seems to fulfill all of these, but it's only momentary the same way alcohol and other substances have momentary relief. As a matter of fact, there are many things that we use to create temporary peace, freedom, and power. Yelling feels like a powerful way to get your point across, but the results tend to vary in the final outcome. Yell at people long enough, and they will leave us alone, but they also don't want to be around us when the time comes.

I remember coming home and having all the kids shout, "Daddy's home!" charging to meet me with a swarm of hugs, playful wrestling, and lots of loud noise. At that moment, I felt like running away. All I wanted was peace and quiet, and not be needed for just one minute. Truthfully it was more like I needed to be left alone for the rest of the week.

I was home every night, didn't go hanging with the boys and from the outside seemed like a good dad. But, I yelled a lot. I spanked too often for the simple infraction of being a kid and it really felt like a bit of me was dying every day. But that's what happens when unavailable for six days out of seven.

Disconnection was my tool and looking back now on how things were, it was not the right tool for the job. My kids wanted to be with me. They wanted to get everything they can from dad while he's home. It felt like I just needed some stress relief, but really I was afraid of failing and having my family find out that dad didn't have what it takes.

At the core of disconnection is the fear of being found out. Not anything bad necessarily, but many of us live with the belief that we're not good enough. Often people feel like they are just barely hanging on. I literally wrote the book on having fun called "Fundamental." While researching that book I discovered the benefits of having fun, but there is a dark side as well. When fun becomes our drug of choice to cover over the emotions that keep us stuck, then it's not the best prescription.

Some men use exercise and recreation as a way to hide. The old cliché of dad going golfing Saturday morning while mom sits at home driven nuts by the kids isn't so cliché. I have many friends that just can't stop going and doing, and it's just a tool to stay busy. To keep from having to spend time in the awkward embrace of connection.

I am all for physical exercise and having outlets away from the family, but the desire to disconnect or run from what's going on at home can be hidden by good things. The top places that men tend to hide from connection are by working, challenging themselves physically, hobbies, and spending time connecting with other men. All of these things are good things. It's less about the action than it is about the purpose.

A few years ago I competed in an Ironman race in Lake Tahoe. When taking on something like that, there is no way to hide from training. It takes between 20-30 hours of training weekly to be prepared for the single greatest physical challenge that I had ever attempted. Between working 40 hours, and training 30 hours, there isn't much time to be with the family. Many of the men that I ran with began to have marriage problems, and some of them ended up divorced because of it. Yikes!

I was actually able to increase connection during my training time, and my family was in full support. What was the difference? The main thing was to do my training when the family didn't need me around. I sacrificed my own sleep, cut into some work hours, and made my family part of the journey. I wouldn't even have started unless they were on board. I remember sitting everyone down and asking their permission to take some extra time to myself for 3-4 months. Then I would run after the kids went to bed and I would swim before work. The only time that the family really suffered from was my Saturday morning pancake ritual. Saturday mornings were my "brick" days, so I biked 50+ miles then ran 4-8miles which took a long time. Except, I always made it home in time to coach the kids' soccer games.

How to tell if our activities are good or part of hiding from home is to look at when they happen and which we prioritize. As an example, I love to surf and sometimes you have to go when the tide and wind are right. That doesn't always lend it's self to happening at the best time. What that looks like for me is I make sure that the family feels prioritized. I won't always go, sometimes I decide to hang out with the kids. Sometimes, it means that we go to the beach as a family and I don't get to surf. And, I wouldn't have it any other way. My family is the most important part of my life.

Kids are an excellent test for connection. It's sometimes difficult to determine if leaving is ok, or if staying is necessary. I look at my kids' behavior. If everyone is crazy and acting out then typically, that means my wife and I need to connect. If just one or two of the kids are in a funk, then I know that they need dad time. Kids wear their emotions externally so learning to read their behavior is an excellent tool for becoming a man the way that God sees us.

It takes courage to connect with people deeply, and even more courage to connect with the ones closest to us because they know how to really make it hurt. They know our deepest secrets and wounds. Often it's easier to hang out with friends than our own family. It's time for the Godmade man to show up and be the honest representation of God the father.

Connection is why Jesus died on the cross, and it is what was lost in the Garden of Eden. Adam walked with God in the cool of the day. When they ate of the fruit, there was a barrier that was created. Men indeed died that day, but not a physical death but an emotional one. I talk with my dad about different things, and when I need advice, he's a good one to call. If we didn't have the relationship we have and he wasn't available to me, that would be a sad thing. My dad is an amazing man, but the Creator of the Universe he is not. Adam one day was in intimate connection with the Alpha and Omega and the next day was supporting himself by the sweat of his brow. It wasn't until Jesus' sacrifice on the cross that we were finally returned to the place that Adam was.

It's easy to see how disconnection is one of the single most significant causes of pain in the world. Man's struggle to become self-reliant and scratch their existence out. In the process, fathers become self-focused and disconnect as a survival mechanism. In survival mode, children can feel more like an anchor dragging us down than joy and honor that they really are. I'm speaking to the extremes, but there were many days that this opinion wasn't too far off from my own truth.

My love didn't ever waver for my kids. I would have died for any of them if I had to. At that time though, if I had to sit through another parent-teacher meeting, it might have been the end of me. The main difference now is how my kids received love. Back then, they received my grouchiness, pushing them away, and hiding from them. I was teaching them what dad's love feels like, which is pretty sad to even write about. The reality was that my heart had been turned away from them by stress and fear.

TURNING THE HEART

"He will restore the hearts of the fathers to their children and the hearts of the children to their fathers, so that I will not come and smite the land with a curse." (Mal. 4:6)

This scripture and the few before it have a lot of prophetic consequence beyond just fathers and sons in the physical. My goal is to highlight just two points that can help us as dads to resolve some of the issues that have been burning for generations. At first glance, I used to reject the notion that my heart was turned away from my kids. I assumed this scripture was talking about other loser dads. Then one day I had a revelation about my actions and what they communicated to the family.

First, the turning of the fathers hearts toward their children comes before the children turn their hearts back to the fathers. The second part is a bit deeper than a willingness to sacrifice for our kids. A heart turned away has to do with vulnerability and connection.

I see this a lot in regards to marriage. One spouse will turn their heart away from the other, then no matter what is said or done there is no reconciliation. It's the same with kids and dads. When children turn their hearts from dad reconciliation is almost impossible. Most of the time as fathers we only see our kids turn away from us and don't realize that we initiated the turning.

When I get a new hobby or start something fun, I tend to go all in. Surfing is a new passion of mine, and I spend time on websites learning about surfboard shapes and watch videos to learn how to read the tide. I surf whenever I get the chance, and I find joy in it. I have effectively turned my heart towards surfing, and the fruit of that is my attention, money, and time go towards it. I used to play soccer a lot and loved to do that, and I still do. However, since I was in a motorcycle accident the ligaments in my ankle are mostly destroyed, and rehab is probably years in the making. What that caused me to do is to turn my heart toward something else.

I don't love playing soccer any less now, but I also haven't bought any new equipment to play in over a year. My heart has turned away from soccer and toward surfing. The fruit of that is evident in how I spend my life.

It's the same for my kids. My heart had turned away to focus on myself because I was desperate. I was so focused on my own pain, stress, and needs that I didn't realize that my heart had turned away from my family. Now that my heart is turned back, the evidence is in how I spend my time. I will always choose to hang out with family over any other activity.

I want to highlight the point that my love for the kids never changed. I always loved them with every fiber of my being. My actions, however, were not consistent with being vulnerable with them and there was definitely a lack of connection. When in relationship, any negative action toward the kids actually causes personal pain. If I need to discipline them, it literally hurts my heart. Before it felt like I was being a good parent by raising them up in a Godly way and teaching them how to act right.

The truth is that most of us don't have a psychology degree with a focus on childhood development before becoming a parent. I've only learned some basic surface level psychology about children, their ages, and how they are capable of responding, and it changed a lot of how I parent. However, the most significant change didn't come from a technique but merely to have an open heart toward my kids.

My focus began to shift to a place where I was really interested in every aspect of their hilarious day. Being genuinely interested in how Darth Vader managed to survive a T-Rex attack was a new thing for me. Yes, I do want to play Legos for 3 1/2 minutes then run around in circles for 2 min then get something to eat.

Phase two is the lightning-quick speed at which kids turn their heart towards the people who are showing them love. My wife even got a little jealous of how the kids want dad sometimes when they would have wanted her before. After many years of them only wanting mom, it was my honor to be wanted in times when they need comfort or something to eat or whatever. She had a little feeling of loss from the shift in attention. Fortunately, I had also turned my heart back toward her as well, so my previous lack of loving communication was now in abundance. Valuing connection and learning how to be vulnerable has radically shifted our household.

Connection is the key that unlocked the door to my heart and allowed us to live the way we do now. I'm still growing and learning what is right and what isn't, but having a home where people feel safe emotionally to let me know when I'm being hurtful or selfish is a great thing. Connection brings freedom, peace, and empowerment to those we are in relationship with.

WHAT TO DO

I remember being confused as to what connection really means. My wife wanted to connect, and I was supposed to fight for connection with my kids. As far as I was concerned, sitting and talking equaled connection. Talking with Nissa was always easy, so we talked often. I enjoyed talking to my kids, so there was a lot of "connecting" going on in my mind.

The truth is, connection is what happens when one open heart communicates with another open heart either verbally or non-verbally. Talking with my family, and even spending time with them alone does not equal connection. Because my wife didn't feel safe to be vulnerable with me and my kids were nervous about how I would react to them, their hearts were closed off to me.

How I was able to finally connect started with a choice to love the ones I loved. Renewing my mind on the truth that my favorite people in the world were in the room with me. The ones who supported me the most, and wanted the best for me were also the ones who I had pushed away. Honestly, in the beginning, it was something that had to be remembered daily. I would repeat in my mind and even out loud sometimes how much I loved each one of them.

My first born, Ezekiel, loves me so much. I am his hero. Every crushing thing I said and did would push him away, and still, he would keep coming back. He is relentless when it's time to get something that he wants. And, he wants me.

Glory is my only girl and the apple of my eye. No one loves more than her. Even when her tears were because of me, her heart was always open. My girl thinks her dad is the best man in the world. How could I let her down!

My second son Luke brings our family so much joy. During my awakening, he was just a baby, but even then his smile would light up the room. Luke is a vital part of our family, and I can't let him experience the self-made version of me.

Micah wasn't born yet during my transformation, and the evidence of our connection is apparent. He doesn't have the father wound that the other kids needed to heal from. He is continuously open-hearted toward us all. His warrior spirit has a place in our home without shame.

These are just some examples of what I would repeat almost daily. It's part of renewing the mind, speaking the truth and leaving out the circumstantial evidence. When our mind is full of beliefs that are not rooted in truth, then the interpretation of circumstances is wrong. Everything that I believed about the people in my life was wrong simply because my base of understanding was not rooted in truth.

The more we press into the truth of our family's love for us the more our heart opens toward them. An open heart is free from uncertainty and is available to connect fully. Having a heart that is partially open does not allow for simple things like talking and quality time to add to connection. In fact often times it creates more relationship strain because the desire for open connection is not being met.

Turning our heart toward the ones we love by renewing our mind is step one. Putting the renewed mind into action is step two. Discover things that are important to each member of the family then do them. Play their game, take them to the park, spend one-on-one time, find ways to communicate love verbally and non-verbally. Then hug and kiss the the shame right off of them.

It's important to remember that connection and disconnection are both a choice. We get one chance to be the husband that our wife thought she was marrying and the dad our kids need us to be. They are only five or twelve or sixteen once. There is no do-over for parents. This is why it's so crucial that we unleash the man that God created us to be.

> I always choose connection when I want to disconnect.

What can I do to choose connection today?

CHAPTER 12

DAD FAILURES

AND WHOEVER RECEIVES ONE SUCH CHILD IN MY NAME RECEIVES ME
MATTHEW 18:5

I have felt like a failure more times than I can count. Sometimes people will tell me that I'm a good dad. I used to think, "If only you knew how I really am you wouldn't say such things." However, the compliments come as a result of how my children act. People see well behaved happy children who are respectful of each other and those around and say, "Good job dad."

The truth is that our children's behavior is a result of how we parent them. All kids are good kids until we screw them up. There are many bad behaviors that my kids have learned from me. They really drink up our failures like a sponge. It's because everything we do to children is communicating love, even negative things.

As a life coach, I have helped people break free from all kinds of self-deprecating behaviors. The story is pretty much always the same. "What lie do you believe about self-love that was modeled to you as a child." My own challenges have come from a skewed perspective of an 8-year-old kid who believed, "I'm the only one that I can count on." My parents had their own challenges, but as a kid, we think everything is our fault. The memory of a preteen is not sufficiently rooted in facts either, it's slightly out of whack and does not have the benefit of complete rational thought until adulthood.

Our challenges and failures as dads will without a doubt contribute to our kids' miss behaviors. The good news is that kids have short memories and are very moldable. When I see my kids acting in a way that I don't like, it's probably because of how I taught them to be. Yes, my wife ads her own stuff to the mix but I can see myself in them very easily.

Be encouraged, it's never too late to get it right. I know several people who had strained relationships with their kids for decades. They change their attitudes, have a contrite heart and then humble themselves. Many strained father relationships have been restored this way. Better is obviously to get it right while they are as young as possible and avoid years of pain. With God nothing is impossible.

I have four kids, and they are all opposites in many ways. I don't even know how it's possible to have four opposites, but they pull it off. With that many different personalities, it's not easy to get it right with each one. With Micah, I need to pause and listen to his perspective. The kid is four years old but already has a strong desire to be heard. I get it, I'm the same way. Luke is my second son and loves to be lost in his own world so I have to make sure he's paying attention before any discipline comes to him or he will miss it. Glory is my only girl, and she is so tender that all I have to do is give her a cross look and she'll start crying. If she thinks I'm disappointed it is devastating, so I need to make sure to reassure her that I am proud of her. My oldest boy Ezekiel got the brunt of my bad parenting. I'm still trying to undo some of the damage I've done with him, but he is impressive at wanting to get things right. Sometimes with him, I have to spend more time celebrating his mistakes, so he realizes the value of trying something new regardless of how things turn out.

It's not fun to see my failures in the kids, but it is to God's glory for me to seek out how to get it right with them. Since allowing my wife to help point out my mistakes it has been great for the kids. They are little mirrors, and I can see where I need to change. Their attitudes and actions are gifts for me to become more of a Godmade dad.

CHILDHOOD DEVELOPMENT

There is a common belief that kids are little adults perpetuated by the church to help create obedient followers. Until a child begins abstract thinking about 11-13 however, they are concrete thinkers; cause and effect. "I touch the fire, I get burned" is often how they learn. Experiential learning is about as far as they can go with understanding consequences. A dumb question for a 6-year-old is, "What were you thinking?". They just do stuff and watch what happens because it's part of their development.

Parents can slowly work to help them be more safe or careful based on development. If we're looking for our kids to make smart choices, then we will have to wait until their brain is fully developed around 23-25 years old. Children are little people with their own identities and ideas, but they do not get the full benefit of rational, critical thought until they are beyond college age.

Even though this is by no means a parenting book, it is essential to have a little knowledge to help get things right. Psychologist Erik Ericksen studied childhood development and came up with the five phases that kids go through until adulthood. These five phases really helped me to get past some feelings of failure and learn how to deal with my own kids.

TRUST VS. MISTRUST: BIRTH TO ABOUT 18 MONTHS

Infants are learning that they can trust people. My oldest son used to give everyone he met the major stare down. They have one goal, which is to survive. Food, safety, warmth, are all of primary concern. Infants trust Mom easiest because they're still connected physically, but they are not sure about Dad yet. When we respond to their crying with care and attention, they get the message that we are safe. Allowing infants to cry it out can cause feelings of anxiety and fear. Their baby mind may see the world as unpredictable. If infants are treated cruelly or their needs are not met appropriately, they will likely grow up with a sense of mistrust for people in the world.

AUTONOMY VS. SHAME/DOUBT: 1.5 - 3

The toddler phase is full of exploration. They are learning like sponges and finding out about cause and effect. This is when they start knocking over towers and also start wanting to be helpful. Food choice, toy selection, and clothing preference begin to show up. The toddler's primary goal is to learn how to be autonomous. Shame and doubt are the emotions that they are fighting. They want to do it themselves, from pouring their own glass of milk to buttoning their own clothes. If denied the opportunity to choose what outfit they want to wear regardless of its appropriateness this could be when they start to develop low self-esteem and have feelings of shame.

INITIATIVE VS. GUILT: 3 - 6

By the time kids get to this pre-school phase they are ready to start their own games and know how to take control of their world. Four years old is about the time that my stories start of the kids doing crazy things on their own. They understand how to have social interactions and are learning the rules of engagement for playing with others. Their big challenge in this age range is learning initiative versus guilt. Playing with other kids, and learning that biting someone might get them to drop the toy, but it will also have your friend swooped up by their parent and the game is over. Exploration is important, and they must be allowed to make mistakes without corporal punishment. This is literally the age when kids decide if their initiative is good or bad. They are learning how to be responsible for their own lives like feeding themselves and learning to tie shoes or ride a bike.

Feeling a sense of ambition and responsibility through initiative happens when parents allow a child to explore within safe limits. Supporting a child's decision and helping them clean up their messes without condemnation is key to developing healthy initiative. It's part of building their self-confidence, and feelings of purpose. If kids are stifled by over controlling parents or failing too many times can develop feelings of guilt.

INDUSTRY VS. INFERIORITY: 6 - 12

Elementary school offers the opportunity for kids to get support from their peers and learn about how their ideas fit in the real world. The main feeling is industry vs. inferiority. There is a lot of learning where they fit in the social structure, and they compare themselves to teammates other kids. Schools have done a horrible job of helping nurture industry and use the fear of inferiority to keep kids inline. It's unfortunate, but this is the phase where we lose our creativity. If things go well and are supported, they will learn to be happy with their accomplishments in sports, school work, family life, and social activities. If they are not encouraged then they begin to feel inadequate and it may stick with them the rest of their lives. Dads and sports are a crucial role in this stage. It's not about celebrating mediocracy, but more supporting through the failures as a way of learning how to get it right. If teenagers and young adults exhibit signs of feeling inadequate, it all points back to this phase.

> "All children are born artists, the problem is to remain an artist as we grow up" - Picasso

IDENTITY VS. ROLE CONFUSION: 12 - 18

Developing a sense of self is an adolescent's main goal. The big questions are asked during this phase, "What do I want to do with my life?" and "Who am I?" They are literally discovering where they fit in this world. Often our plans for them create a struggle as they are discovering if they want to follow in our footsteps or go off on their own. Exploring other ideas, and setting goals is part of becoming an adult. Stifling their own expression can lead to role confusion and an "identity crisis." Learning that they are valuable for what they bring to the table is part of creating a positive adolescent time. Creating a strong sense of identity is critical, and is one of the reasons that youth tend to gravitate towards groups. The jocks, goths, and motorheads are an adolescent's attempt to find where they fit in this world. Having a strong sense of identity will help them get through this phase with their beliefs intact. Controlling parents can often create rebellion, but successful parenting at this phase is all about creating a sense of personal responsibility and the freedom to make their own decisions, consequences and all. A teenager who is unsuccessful at this stage will often have identity issues as an adult and struggle to find themselves throughout their adulthood.

MAKING A MESS

I'm pretty sure I've messed up a lot of those. Fortunately, love covers a multitude of sins. Whenever I've blown it, I make sure to lather the kids with love. It's not essential to try to "cover" my mistakes, in fact the kids have appreciated my honesty with letting them know how I messed up. But, even in that failure, there is an opportunity to grow together, and kids respond well to it.

Receiving parenting instructions before I was called Dad would have been nice, but unfortunately, I only had "monkey see, monkey do" examples. I had a dad, the grandpas, and men in the church for examples. Then there is tv, movies, and the worldly perspective. If I add in an authoritarian version of God the Father to my list of "how to parent for the self-made dad," it's no surprise that I blew it often. We are all trying our best, but like boxing, everyone has a plan until they get hit in the mouth. My parenting plan flew out the window the first time I heard the kid scream.

My youngest son is probably the best example of Ephesians 6:4 to me. *"Fathers, do not provoke your children to anger, but bring them up in the discipline and instruction of the Lord."* At four years old he really doesn't understand why I'm telling him to stop licking his shoe. All he knows is that dad is making him stop doing what he wants to do. No matter what I say, he'll get mad. He shouts, stomps his feet and flops on the floor with a sigh of desperation. As kids get older, they respond differently and have different needs.

In Colossians 3:21 it says something similar, *"Fathers, do not exasperate your children so that they will not lose heart."* I've seen this first hand. My middle son Luke is such an amazing kid, but even he sometimes will feel like he's not being recognized. There have been times where I have been irritated with his actions and broke his spirit by my words. Fortunately, I've learned how to clean up my own messes and go make things right with him.

An apology from Dad is an excellent start towards setting the record straight about how we really feel about them. Letting our kids see that even Superman has failures actually gives them hope. Children believe that everything is their fault even when being mistreated, so it's important to take ownership of our misbehaviors in reaction to whatever it was that they did. After connecting to their heart, then there is freedom and openness to learning what part they played in the problem, and how we can both do better next time.

Failures as a parent are not avoidable. From learning how each child needs to be dealt with to overcoming our own old stories, we can be sure that mistakes will be made. Our job is to do better next time. Understanding how God fathers us through love and freedom will help get us closer to becoming the Godmade Dad that we want to be. The scriptures are valuable to help guide our skills, but understanding the heart of God for us will bring clarity that will genuinely help us parent our kids with the fullness of love.

SPARE THE ROD, SPOIL THE CHILD

My goal is to be the dad that God created me to be. I don't much care what the world suggests is the proper way to parent, nor do I care what the church thinks is the right way to parent. I am looking for God's design to being a dad. As such, there are learning opportunities from history and modern understanding. To spank or not to spank, time-outs and shame-parenting, even the no-discipline approach have been suggested to me as a dad. Some from the church, and others from social media and their clever videos and shaming comments from people who don't know the first thing about me. It is very confusing.

I will not attempt to suggest one form of discipline over another here because that is a debate for the ages, but I want to highlight some points that will help us approach discipline the way that God intended. Even though I still get this wrong often, and my parenting is a work in progress, I can tell you that my kids have expressed their appreciation to me for how I am with them.

The evidence of my past ways is apparent in my oldest son who is a good boy who learned how not to piss off dad. I would much rather see the evidence of good kids who know how to receive love from dad. This is the mark of a Godmade Dad, one who loves his kids openly, and receives love from his kids easily. Just the other day we were walking down the street as a family, I was a little irritated and hot, and Micah shouts out from behind, "I love you, daddy!" A lady sitting on the bench eating her lunch almost started crying she was so moved by that; I was moved too.

The point of discipline is to guide our children to be loving, Christ-centered adults who know the fullness of their identity in God and to have a productive joy-filled life. Simple, right? Thus, is the challenge of parenting. We are only going to be able to do our very best, and the rest will have to be on the kids to sort out on their own.

King Solomon offered some great advice, but his scriptures on discipline have caused a lot of controversy, *"Whoever spares the rod hates their children but the one who loves their children is careful to discipline them. - Proverbs 13:24"* At least 8 other times in proverbs he writes something similar, *"Do not withhold discipline from a child; if you punish them with the rod, they will not die. Proverbs 23:13"*. The other scriptures are not much more encouraging. *"Folly is bound up in the heart of a child, but the rod of discipline will drive it far away. Proverbs 22:15"*.

Even though I am tempted to explain what these scriptures mean, I would rather talk about the heart of God towards us. Then we can explore a bit about my take on this section of scripture. God is love.

God is good, and he is in a good mood. King David wrote this in *Psalm 136:1, "Give thanks to the LORD, for He is good, For His lovingkindness is everlasting."* We are not lead by an authoritarian who is hell-bent on punishment. The point of discipline is to correct errant behaviors. The purpose of punishment is to create fear by which people are manipulated into "good behavior." This is how the law works, to force people to behave or be punished.

God didn't create a law to punish man. Exodus chapter twenty is where we first see any notion of law; however, these are statements of greatness. It's not written, "do not have," but rather, "You will have." The original 10 commandments held no punishment in them. There was no, "follow these or go to hell" statements when Moses descended with the stone tablets.

Here's Jesus' take on the law and the prophets. *Matthew 22:37-40, "Jesus replied: "'Love the Lord your God with all your heart and with all your soul and with all your mind.' This is the first and greatest commandment. And the second is like it: 'Love your neighbor as yourself.' All the Law and the Prophets hang on these two commandments."* He read them as statements of loving and being loved. There is no fear of death or punishment.

Hell is a place completely separated from God. The best description for it is a lake of fire because we were made to be one with him. It's not a fairytale land with devils and pitchforks, but a waterless place where those incarcerated are in complete lack of every need, always. It was not created for us, but to remove the deceiver from ever attempting to be the fake version of God again.

The fear of hell is not a ploy of God to keep us in line but was perpetuated by the early church to create obedient followers. It's impossible for humans to stay in line, and therefore God designed a way to avoid that place forever. By the greatest love story ever written; *John 3:16, "For God so loved the world, that He gave His only begotten Son, that whoever believes in Him shall not perish, but have eternal life."* Fear of hell is removed from the table forever.

Being the dad that God intended means we strive to eliminate the fear of punishment from our tool belt. Ultimately it's not on us whether or not our children have fear, but we can help. For some reason when I'm disciplining my children, if I don't see a contrite spirit then I tend to keep going until I do. In my error, that means yelling or being scary. When I'm getting it right, it looks like pouring love on them.

Here's an example of loving discipline. "I can see that you were just trying to be funny, but some things are not allowed because it hurts other people. Because of your actions, your sister doesn't want to play with you right now. She loves you and knows that you are a kind boy and loves her too. Right now you will have to play by yourself until she feels safe to be with you. If you tell her you are sorry and show her that you made a mistake, then I'm sure she will want to keep playing." It doesn't have to look exactly like that, but there is no fear of punishment. The fact that the child is removed is a cause and effect of negative behavior.

That is how God's discipline works for us. If we make a mess, then we are responsible for cleaning it up. If I treat my wife poorly, the consequence will be a lack of connection and will likely create chaos in the home. It's a cause and effect. Fortunately, kids can understand cause and effect from a very young age, so discipline from about 2 years old on is a good thing.

Going back to Solomon's approach to avoiding spoiled children, understand that whether the rod of correction looks like a firm hand or chair in the corner of the room the purpose is not supposed to be punishment. If it creates fear, then perhaps a different tool should be used. Even though I personally have used spanking in the past, I don't feel it's a good tool for the Godmade dad. There are perhaps sometimes where it could be used, but definitely few and far in between. Timeout is another one that can be to good effect, but this has been proven to be worse than spanking psychologically. It depends on the intention, and if it's used to shame kids or create disconnection.

There is a video circulating the internet where the woman is suggesting that timeout should not be used at all. Even though there is thoughtfulness behind what she is trying to say, her suggestion is to ditch discipline in favor of empathy. The problem is that as adults, all actions cause a response. Good behaviors cause good reactions, and poor actions cause adverse reactions. Discipline is a way for kids to begin to connect the dots on "my actions impact those around me."

With four kids, I can tell you that there are times the only solution is to separate everyone for a few minutes so we can come back together and work through the problem. It's all about age-appropriate actions. From 0-1.5 according to Erik Ericksen children are in the "trust" phase. Discipline during this time is almost useless. The best solution is the distraction method. 1.5-3 they are dealing with being their own person vs. shame. This is the danger zone for time out and shame parenting. They are just trying to be their own person. 3-5 they are testing boundaries and doing bad things intentionally. This is an excellent simple discipline phase. 5-12 is where they can handle time out as a pre-discussed time to reflect on their actions and how it impacted the rest of us. ALL discipline should be done with empathy, but no discipline will be a disaster.

Solomon's point about sparing the rod is to highlight how beneficial discipline is to help children turn into productive members of society. We must remember to discipline with the heart of God as our guide. Being a work in progress is ok. I always try to talk with my kids after the situation has passed and we can both talk openly about it. Even the four-year-old has a measure of understanding once his rage has left.

God's grace can be defined as divine empowerment to change. The same grace that brought us into the loving embrace of the father is the same grace that can allow us to get past our shortcomings. Allowing God to be part of our journey to become a good dad is really the easiest way to get what we're after.

Raise up children in the way they should go, and they will not depart from it all the days of their life. It's time to stop failing our children. We can parent with purpose and represent the love of Abba to our kids. The bible is not an excuse to be a mean parent. Reading scripture with the perspective that God is good and he is proud of us will produce a better result in our lives, and in our children's future.

> My kids' behavior reflect my attitude.

Write a note to your kids and say whatever is in your heart.

CHAPTER 13

THE SACRIFICIAL DAD

LIKE ARROWS IN THE HANDS OF A WARRIOR ARE CHILDREN BORN IN ONE'S YOUTH.

PSALM 127:4

My first reaction was anger, then sadness, then I started to rant. For days I was upset about this one image. It wasn't political, socially charged, or any other common blood boiler. What I saw was the silhouette of a child and a dad. The child was missing one puzzle piece, and the dad was handing the child that missing piece from himself. The dad was missing most of his puzzle pieces as it was common practice for him to sacrifice for his kid. The tagline read, "parenting is sacrifice."

Kids do not equal sacrifice. I'm not suggesting that as parents we don't go above and beyond for them, but there is a common belief which kills the hearts of men everywhere that children equal sacrifice. The directive is to give of yourself over and over until there is nothing left. Pour out and make a place for your children to accomplish what you couldn't. Do that and die happy, having never fulfilled any of our own passions and dreams, as long as the kids got what they needed.

What a horrible example to leave for our children. "Here's how to be a good dad kid, give up everything you've ever dreamed of and forget about taking care of yourself because your life is required by someone else." We give, and give, and give until we are a shell of who we used to be. All in the name of trying to be a good dad.

Movies and tv shows praise the super dad. That guy who does it all, runs a successful business, is at all the kid's games, takes the family camping once a year, and lives a life dedicated to the rearing of his family. Then In those same films, the dad will have a mid-life crisis or start to lose it toward everyone.

Living the kind of life that is dedicated to sacrifice will raise adults that leave home with the intention of being nothing like their parents. Those kids will resent their parents or worse feel guilty for putting them through so much. Who knows how far and wide the ramifications are for raising kids to believe that they ruined our hopes and dreams.

In essence, sacrifice implies that we gave up something to be with our children. It sounds loving on the surface, and there are times where we choose to give up time golfing to watch 8-year-olds run around a soccer field, but to be the example of a good dad we need something better. There is a higher calling, and it takes strength and determination. The better way is to become the man that God created us to be.

The scripture from 1 Samuel 15 "obedience is better than sacrifice" isn't talking about being a dad, but it's evidence that sacrifice is not the best way. Samuel was prophesying about how all the sacrifices in the world cannot equal the value of listening to the voice of the Lord. Essentially, getting it right is better than repentance.

God's original design was for connection. Jesus' sacrifice on the cross was the second option. Sacrifice as a means for redemption is what happens after sin. Sacrifice is for redemption not for showing love.

The correct word is service. We are in service to our families. We get to go out of our way to support them. It is our honor to wash their feet as Jesus did with Peter.

To be a "good dad," it's time to slay the sacrificial lamb strategy and move forward to the listening to God's voice strategy. God calls us to lead our family. No one wants to follow a broken leader who has given up on their dreams and visions. Better is to be the shining hero which kids believe their dad is already.

The purpose of a good father is to guide his family to their own greatness. There is a scene from the movie Rocky Balboa where Rocky is talking to his grown-up son. It's the part where we get the best quote, "Let me tell you something you already know. The world ain't all sunshine and rainbows. It's a very mean and nasty place, and I don't care how tough you are it will beat you to your knees and keep you there permanently if you let it. You, me, or nobody is gonna hit as hard as life. But it ain't about how hard ya hit. It's about how hard you can get hit and keep moving forward. How much you can take and keep moving forward. That's how winning is done!" Rocky's son had just finished telling him how hard it was living in his shadow; to try to measure up to his greatness. He was expressing his heart of feeling not good enough.

What we know from all the Rocky movies is that the character really loved his family and seemed to sacrifice everything for them. Even his boxing was to support his family and give them a good life. In this moment of vulnerability between a father and a son, he learned that all that sacrifice didn't teach his son the most valuable lesson of all. That every person has what it takes if they will just believe it.

At a critical moment in the big match, Rocky is knocked down for the umpteenth time, and while laying on the canvas, he thinks to himself, "What is it you said to the kid? It ain't about how hard you hit, It's about how hard you can get hit and keep moving forward. Get up!" At that moment, he was doing what every great dad in history has done, lead by example. It's our example that teaches our kids how they should be.

Words are almost meaningless when compared to actions. It's being the example of greatness which teaches the most important lessons. And here's the kicker for greatness, it's not about the outcome but the process. If someone is wealthy but didn't earn it, then we call them lucky but don't want to learn from them. It's the ones who struggled, battled, and came out victorious that become mentors.

I had a similar moment once. My wife and kids had sacrificed a few months of Dad-time so I could train for the Ironman 70.3 Lake Tahoe triathlon race. It was toward the end of the race, and I had done relatively well compared to what people expected of me, but exhaustion began to take hold. With about 12 miles left to run my right knee went out on me, and I hit the ground. It took a minute to gain composure, but I came up with a strategy to keep going. Walk the hills and limp run the flats. Everything was going fine then two miles later my right knee went out. I collapsed in a heap, a beaten man. Tears flowed, thoughts of quitting swirled and I really thought about kicking out of the race.

Just when all hope was lost, a picture of my family cheering at the finish line for a husband and father that would never show up flashed into my mind's eye. I couldn't quit, and just like Rocky I thought, "Get up!" I couldn't let my kids know that it was ok to quit when things got hard. They would understand that I tried my best, but it would always be defeat. Sometimes it's ok to lose, but not today. At that moment I thought about my oldest son Ezekiel and how strong he is, mentally. I began to chant, "Ezekiel wouldn't quit..." and pulled myself to my feet. I kept running the remaining ten miles, holding my family in mind.

When I crossed the finish line battered, bruised, and exhausted there were only feelings of love and admiration. My wife and kids were proud, and I was proud. The thing that made it all worthwhile though was the example that was left for my kids. I taught them that there is nothing they can't accomplish if they would try and push through when things get hard. No amount of sacrifice could ever teach that.

One could argue that it was a sacrifice for me to dig deep when I felt like quitting. The truth is that I didn't have to give up anything to be the example. It was challenging and painful, but in the end, I added to myself, not detracted. This is the difference.

We are not a piggy bank for our kids to tap into when things get tough. We are a compass that points the direction of their own greatness. Sometimes that looks like giving up things that we want, but mostly it is being the best example of what it looks like to be great.

I believe the same desire to champion our kids can cause the position of sacrifice. How many of us wouldn't take a bullet for our children? I know that I would without hesitation. "Greater love has no one than this: to lay down one's life for one's friends." John 15:13. We have a love for our kids deeper than anything else, including our own lives. Since most of us have a measure disappointment with where our lives are at compared to where we dreamed them to be, it's no surprise then that we do whatever we can to help our kids avoid failure. The right tool is to be in service to our family.

TO CHAMPION IS BETTER THAN SACRIFICE

The working title of this book before any writing started was Champion because the concept of championing our families to their own greatness is the call of all men. Nothing stirs our hearts up like stories of great men doing great things to either save their family or be an example for them. The movies Cinderella Man, Braveheart, Kingdom of Heaven comes to mind. All are films that show men doing great things as part of a lasting legacy for the love of their family. In the case of Cinderella Man, he fought so his wife and kids wouldn't starve to death. Braveheart was about both revenge for the love that was stolen and to lead his "clan" and all of Scotland into freedom, and in the Kingdom of Heaven, it was the extension of the example left behind by his father.

Regardless of choice in movies or the examples that the world gives us, the most excellent example is always God. David was not great because he killed Goliath but because of the character that drove him to fight Goliath to begin with. David, a man after God's own heart, was angry over this Philistine insulting his people and more importantly his God. Before this meeting David had been anointed as King over Israel, and even though Saul was currently in charge, David was the right man for the job.

At that moment, David became a champion, and his stories and accomplishments guide us while on our own journey. From learning how to treat the Lord's anointed even when they are seeking our death, to how to worship God with reckless abandon. The actions of David speak volumes more than the actual words ever could. This is how we should be for our kids, a man after the heart of the King of Kings.

During the Renaissance period a champion was someone who had done great feats in battle or sport and represented a region or district. They became part of the defining identity for those people regardless of their social class. I visited a medieval town in Italy called Sienna which still races horses for their districts every year. Each section of the city is divided into the area of their champion. Statues of a dragon, rhinoceros, a shell or whatever their symbol is, adorn the street lights and houses of that section. Their champion has a home on the corner of their district with information about who he is and what he represents for them. This champion is the identity of his people.

It was the job of this hero to fight on behalf of their king or regent. Whether in combat or sport they were the embodiment of the king's wishes and honor. They were the physical representation of the spirit of their community.

In Sienna, Italy the people proudly wear their symbol as a badge of honor. My son Luke loves turtles, and we bought a Tortuga badge as a souvenir. The man we purchased it from in broken English said, "I from Tortuga," as he proudly and carefully packaged up our purchase for safe travel.

We are the champion of the King of Kings to our family. They proudly wear us on their sleeves like a badge of honor. "My dad is better than your dad," echoes through the playground of every school across the planet. We are both the hands and feet of God and the spirit of greatness that our kids will use to fight their own battles. Every kid believes that their dad is a superhero.

Every man wants his family to exceed his own success or avoid his failures and for them to have an easier path to that end. The challenge is to be the example of possibility. My ceiling should be my kids' floor, but that's not really how things work. Rarely these days do children follow in their father's footsteps directly. However, the growth that we have and the example we leave behind creates the ceiling.

We have the power to show what is possible. We get to use our authority and community to empower our children on to their own path. *"The heart of a man makes his plans, but the Lord directs his steps." Proverbs 16:9.* The words we speak and the actions we take will either propel them or hinder them.

THE HEART

Most of us don't really know what we want to do or be. There are very few people that feel like they are fulfilling their purpose. If you ask a child though, they will tell you what's on their heart. It can change from week to week, but they know at that moment exactly what they want. My kids want to be professional soccer players right now. Will they achieve that success? There is no way for me to answer that question. If I tell them the likely story that very few people become professional athletes and ground them to reality, am I doing them a favor? All that does is detach them from their hearts. What I do know is that every professional athlete believed that they were the best in the world and never quit on their dream regardless of what other people said. The key is to discover their heart.

The heart of a child believes in possibilities because they don't have any past failures to teach them what they can't do. We are the teachers of what they can and can't do. Our successes and failures teach them, and our attitudes toward their heart teach them. It is not our job to manage their heart, it is our job to discover their heart.

Just like the Lord, we get to help direct their steps. But not toward what we think is possible. It's our job to guide them toward what they believe is possible. What if one of my sons becomes the best surfer of all time? What if my daughter becomes the president of the united states? Or what if they lead a beautiful life of faith, hope, and love with no fame or notoriety. It's not my life, and it's not my job. I have my own shot at life, just like they have theirs. As the champion of the Lord in their life, I get to be the representative of God's possibilities. Luke chapter one verse thirty-seven says, "for nothing will be impossible with God."

Being God's champion feels like a massive responsibility until we understand what He expects from us. Remember, he gave us kids without instructions or qualifications. Why would He do that if he didn't believe that we have what it takes already? God sees us the way he created us, not the way that we created us. He made us champions before we ever succeeded at anything.

We must fight for their hearts. The desires and dreams they have are wild and impossible and world-changing. And with the strength of their father backing up the crazy there's no telling what they will achieve. Dads think about things like, money, future, and responsibility because that is what we were taught. How much more excellent is the adventure of one, who has the complete backing of their father.

After having started several businesses and tried many crazy things of my own, I can say without any hesitation that nothing ever goes according to plan. All final products have gone through an array of changes and modifications. Often the end result looks nothing like the original dream. The famous story of the yellow sticky pad came from people trying to make the strongest glue on the planet. Tesla did not set out to create one of the most significant breakthroughs in battery technology in our generation, they just wanted a cool looking electric car. Electric cars already existed but battery technology needed an upgrade.

When our kids are little, they learn the rules of engagement for life and apply that to everything they do for the rest of their days. "Train up a child in the way he should go, even when he is old he will not depart from it. (Prov 22:6)" is 100% accurate in psychological terms. For example, punish a child every time they do something wrong, and they will learn that trying new things or being first to try new things is bad. As they grow up, there will be a rule in their brain that if they make a mistake that bad things will happen.

My oldest son was naturally cautious as an infant, and as first-time parents everything in the world seemed to want to harm him. We were excellent about keeping him safe. Fast forward to today, and he is very well mannered and doesn't do things that look potentially dangerous. Even if I assure him it's safe, until he can rationalize it in his mind, he will not do it. Our fear of his pain sucked the joy of exploration from his heart.

Fortunately, he was still young when I had my breakthrough, and we have done a good job of encouraging him and healing that wound in his heart. It was my fear that wounded him, not the world. I sometimes go a bit overboard with challenging him to try something that he might fail at so I can support him through it. Again, this falls under the repentance category. Had I been a champion of his heart from the beginning then I would have avoided wounding him that way.

Children do not equal sacrifice, they equal challenge. They challenge us to grow as we challenge them to discover. We challenge them to do better, and they show us how we can follow our own advice. There is no more significant source of growth in a man's life than his child.

> I serve my family
> with joy and freedom.

How can I launch my children into their destiny and greatness?

CHAPTER 14

I BELIEVE IN YOU

GOD HAS ALREADY APPROVED YOUR WORKS.
ECCLESIASTES 9:7

The need for validation is one of the greatest motivators on earth. All of us; men, women, children, teenagers, even babies need to have some form of validation. Some say the need for approval comes from a daddy wound, and others think it's the social conditioning of authority figures like coaches and teachers are to blame. Some psychologists point to parents withholding love when kids don't do things right as a factor, while others suggest rejection, ridicule, or discipline as starting points. Other's believe that perhaps it's just how God created us.

There is no doubting that the need for approval causes a lot of pain in this world. Some studies have shown that as much as 70% of people suffer from imposter syndrome, which is a label to describe the feeling of not having what it takes and if people found out how over our heads we are, then there would be a problem. Approval, validation, acceptance are all buzz words that point to a base human need.

According to Abraham Maslow, there is a hierarchy of personal needs that all people require. The base needs are physiological like food, water, shelter, sleep, clothing, and air. After the base needs are met, a person must feel safe, physically, financially, and most importantly emotionally. The next levels like love, belonging, and esteem becomes a moot point. We will sacrifice our importance, social status, self-respect and the respect of others to make sure the base needs are met.

Whatever the root of all these grown-up problems may be, it's almost irrelevant once someone discovers their identity in Christ. When we know who we are and whose we are, then the need for approval fades away. One of my most significant discoveries was that God created us perfect. I am the son of the King of Kings, and he has given me all authority over the things of this world. Abba gave me the keys to his kingdom because he trusts me!

Our children get a similar sense of belonging, empowerment, and authority when we say, "I believe in you." We are simultaneously giving identity to our kids and representing God's love. The misconception is that dads are the primary example of the character of God the Father to their children. We take the blame for teaching our kids improper versions of who God is because we are not perfect. If the goal, however, is to empower them to discover their own greatness, then we cannot own the responsibility of being God to them.

We represent God's love by giving them the freedom to get things wrong in a safe environment. When we support our children through their mistakes, it communicates that they are in the driver's seat of their own lives and they don't need more approval than they already have. We are not representatives of the identity of God, but rather are representatives of a relationship with the Father. "Son, I am a son like you, and this is how the author and perfecter of my faith will treat me."

When Samuel was directed to anoint the next king of Israel he was instructed to find a man after His own heart. He then anoints David so we can assume that David was a "man after God's own heart." How does an earthly man who is after God's heart treat his children and raise the next king of Israel? There isn't much in the way of how David was as a parent, so we need to turn to the kids. Here's a quick list of David's sons.

THE CHILDREN OF DAVID

1. **Amnon** - David's firstborn, born in Hebron to Ahinoam of Jezreel. Absalom killed him after he raped Absalom's full sister, Tamar.

2. **Kileab** (or Daniel), the second son, whose mother was Abigail from Carmel. He probably died young since there is no record of his life.

3. **Absalom**, the third son, born to Maacah, the daughter of Talmai, king of Geshur. He was killed by Joab (1 Chronicles 3:1-2) after he mounted a rebellion against his aging father, David.

4. **Adonijah,** the fourth son of King David from Haggith (2 Samuel 3:4). He attempted to usurp the throne during the life of David (1 Kings 1:11ff). Solomon had him executed after being warned to remember his place in the line of succession per King David's instruction regarding the crown. 1 Kings 1:32-35; 1:50-53; 2:13-25[3]

5. **Shephatiah**, whose mother was Abital. He was born while his father was still reigning at Hebron

6. **Ithream**, whose mother was Eglah, "David's wife." The expression "wife of David" (II Sam. iii. 5) probably means the favorite wife of David.

THE SONS BORN TO DAVID IN JERUSALEM INCLUDED THE SONS OF BATHSHEBA

7. The infant who died without being named
8. **Shimea**, or Shammua, probably the first surviving child of Bathsheba

9. **Shobab**, from Bathsheba, is one of the three full brothers of Solomon
10. **Nathan** (son of David), Bathsheba the ancestor of Jesus according to the Genealogy of Jesus in Luke 3:31, considered by some to be the maternal line via Heli, possible father of Mary.
11. **Solomon**, Bathsheba, the ancestor of Jesus according to the Genealogy of Jesus in Matthew, often considered to be Joseph's line.

Reading through this list, it seems that David sucked at being a dad with his earlier sons, and started to get things right towards the end of his child-rearing days. There is one caveat, there were different moms involved in each of the six earlier sons, and he had not yet settled down until Bathsheba. Children are a product of their environment, so I want to be clear that the first six were not born in a stable, loving environment but were a product of David, the warrior. The children of Bathsheba were all born in Israel in a seemingly stable environment.

Solomon was the last born to David and ended up being the one that God chose to build His temple and succeed the throne of Israel.

With the prophetic nature of David's life, his children, and his 33-year reign aside we can assume at least one thing that helped shape Solomon to become the man that we read about. David had learned a valuable lesson during the pregnancy of his first son with Bathsheba. Nathan's call for repentance shifted David's heart. He was genuinely grieved about his actions and was willing to give up his own life in payment. It's a good thing God didn't require his life. God is a good father, not a punitive narcissist.

David should give us all hope about what our role is as a father. The king of the greatest nation on earth at the time showed the power of a father's belief in their child in the midst of imperfection.

God knew his heart was good. He had anointed David to be the leader of God's people and put his stamp of approval on him even in the midst of multiple failures.

A result of stepping into the identity of a cherished son of God was evident in David's later children becoming the lineage of Jesus and the successor to the throne of Israel. Solomon was gifted with the task of creating the house of worship and resting place of the presence of God on earth. Not too bad, dad.

Solomon writes about God's belief in us in Ecclesiastes chapter nine verse seven, "Go, eat your food with gladness, and drink your wine with a joyful heart, for God has already approved your works." By the time Solomon comes into the picture, David had already made the heart shift. I assume that one of the lessons that Solomon learned early on was that David believed in him the way that God the Father believes in us. Solomon knew his identity as the son of the king and of the King of Kings. Only a son who understands the fullness of authority could write about having approval even in the midst of mistakes and uncertainty.

Many places in scripture point to God's favor, approval, and thoughts toward us. Somehow though, it doesn't get translated that way when we hear or read it. *"I know what I'm doing. I have it all planned out—plans to take care of you, not abandon you, plans to give you the future you hope for." Jeremiah 29:11 (The Message Bible)*

This is not a free pass to create lawless children, just like grace is not a free pass to sin. Grace can be described as the divine empowerment to change. In the same way, creating an "I believe in you" zone even when the outcome doesn't match gives kids the freedom to get things right.

Mistakes are their own punishment. Traditional parental guidance is to help keep kids on the right track, so they don't experience pain, and more importantly, so the parents don't experience pain. Avoiding pain always leads to more pain. Creating a home system where kids are afraid to fail will always backfire.

Sports are a great example of how fear cripples success. Many times championships were won by the team that, according to the stats, should have lost. The announcers then debate the power of not having anything to prove, having nothing to lose, and the lack of fear. Sometimes young teams are touted for their lack of belief that they should be afraid of the big dogs.

Most of the pain I've suffered in sports have come from being afraid. In football, being afraid to take a hit makes it hurt worse than the belief that I have what it takes. Surfing, I've wiped out more often when fearful of the power of the wave, or the environment I was in. Just looking at the physical side of things, being timid and afraid to fail has caused more pain than any mistakes I've made doing the opposite.

Emotionally it's the same thing. I'm still working on trying to reprogram my older kids to understand that they will not be punished for failing. I was not the best encourager through mistakes early on. The downside to empowering kids to try even when they will likely mess up is some broken dishes and spilled food. The downside to a lack of support though is crippling for a lifetime and creates doubt that is not easily overcome.

It seems easier to be supportive of our children in certain things more than in others. If we don't expect our kid to be a world-class artist, then it's easy to be supportive when our five-year-old draws a picture of a cat, and it looks like a rowboat. Encouraging at that age and in that arena is easy. Now, go to a little kid's soccer game, and parents are shouting at their child to be aggressive and fight for every ball. They are yelling at the referees and putting down the coaches. All of a sudden, the stakes are higher since the kid is going to be a multimillionaire athlete. Now, dad needs to be hard on his child to make sure they have the best start available.

In the end, our desire to support our kids into their greatness causes some very irrational behavior. I personally don't like the everyone gets a trophy atmosphere that exists today, but at the same time, I see how the benefits of it are probably more for the parents to just chill the heck out. The desire to achieve is good, but the tools we choose might not be the most effective. In one of my previous books *FUNdamental: The Transforming Power of Having Fun*, I wrote about the power of enjoyment for growth and success.

As a father, we have the most powerful tool of all, our approval. "I believe in you, and that you have what it takes. Whether or not this coach can see it doesn't matter. You are free to be whomever you want, and if you keep trying hard to be yourself, then great things will happen. Keep going, keep believing, because I believe in you 100% and you will always be good enough to be my son/daughter."

In the past, I have felt responsible for my children's success or lack thereof. I'm not sure that would have been uttered publicly, but being honest with myself now, it was definitely an internal belief. "I want the very best for my kids. They shouldn't have to suffer through what I've struggled with. If they don't just listen to me, then I will force them to do what they are supposed to. It's good for them, so they have no choice but to do what they are told."

Control, manipulation, shaming, and fear are common tools that are used to try to create successful children. In the end, it will only make more men and women who are struggling to gain approval and support the vision of unhealthy and self-focused leaders. The power of belief even in the face of mistakes is the single greatest weapon against self-doubt, lack of personal value, and shame.

Here's the kicker, raising empowered children all starts with personal transformation. It's serious business that we learn the power of who we are in Christ, and whose we are as sons of God. The more we learn that God the father believes in us even while we're still making mistakes, the more it will translate to our children.

SCRIPTURES TO GET OUR BELIEF GOING

"For I know the thoughts I think toward you, says the Lord, thoughts of peace and not of evil, to give you a future and a hope." - Jeremiah 29:11.

"Your eyes saw my substance, being yet unformed. And in Your book they all were written, the days fashioned for me, when as yet there were none of them. How precious also are Your thoughts to me, O God! How great is the sum of them!" - Psalm 139:16-17.

"Are not two sparrows sold for a copper coin? And not one of them falls to the ground apart from your Father's will. But the very hairs of your head are all numbered. Do not fear therefore; you are of more value than many sparrows." - Matthew 10:29-31

"But you are a chosen generation, a royal priesthood, a holy nation, His own special people, that you may proclaim the praises of Him who called you out of darkness into His marvelous light." 1 Peter 2:9.

"Just as He chose us in Him before the foundation of the world, that we should be holy and without blame before Him in love, having predestined us to adoption as sons by Jesus Christ to Himself, according to the good pleasure of His will ..."Ephesians 1:4-5.

"For we are His workmanship, created in Christ Jesus

for good works, which God prepared beforehand that we should walk in them." Ephesians 2:10.

"For this is good and acceptable in the sight of God our Savior, who desires all men to be saved and to come to the knowledge of the truth." 1 Timothy 2:3-4.

MAKING A MESS OF THINGS

Kids do not come with instruction manuals. There is not a handbook given out that directly tells us how to "Dad it up." The bible is full of the mysteries of God, and we can glean wisdom and understanding of how to behave from it, but all that wisdom doesn't automatically pop into our minds and shift things the minute we become a dad.

I was terrified and didn't know it. I was afraid of not having what it takes to be a real man. There was an underlying fear of letting my wife and kids down. On the surface, I didn't have any recognition of these fears, but sitting here many years later I know these beliefs created my world.

Allowing fear to "prove it's self" in my life is agreeing with the enemy and renewing my mind into an inaccurate perspective. Every time something that we're afraid of happening seems to show up it's easy to say, "See, that always happens to me." The solution to proving fear wrong is the willingness to make a mistake.

A lesson I learned years ago came through a friend of mine who was teaching me to play the drums. He said, "If you're going to make a mistake, make it as loud as you possibly can." He was referring to how being afraid to mess up the beat will actually cause mistakes to happen. At that moment, my drumming became much better, and I began to grow exponentially in my ability. The lesson is this, fear of making a mistake more readily causes mistakes to occur.

Kids make mistakes all the time. They are always messing things up it seems. From peeing the bed to falling down and getting hurt. The older they get, the bigger the mistakes. They begin to grow out of certain mistakes while discovering new ones because as they grow, they learn.

Children are constantly doing new things. Walking for the first time, learning to talk, and brushing their teeth are just some basic examples. We could say that they are making a mess through the process of learning how to get things right. There is grace for that.

Becoming a dad for the first time means we are learning something new. It's been challenging to find effective mentoring and role models. There is a learning process that can take a lifetime to master. Ultimately we will fail from time to time. The goal should be, not to fail in the same way over and over. Just like our children, we should be learning and growing and failing forward.

It's time to give ourselves a little grace. Every phase in life is new and different. Our kids behave differently at four than they do at ten. We are in an ever-changing atmosphere which should mean mistakes will be made. Kids forgive easily, forget quickly, and you can guarantee they will make a mess.

Making mistakes will happen, knowing how to clean up after is how to get past them. Even in the cleanup, often there are mistakes because the mess might be new. The crazy thing about trying something new is that things will not go according to plan. We have to give ourselves some grace through the process.

Grace is not the freedom to make a mess whenever we want but is the empowerment to change the behaviors that caused the mess to begin with. Not having eternal consequences beyond the mess allows us the freedom to do things differently, without the fear of future pain or the shame of failure. Our past failures as a father might need a little cleaning up; however, we can be assured that our children are ready to forgive and move on as soon as we're ready to forgive ourselves.

Most of the men I know are really good dads. It's not because I only surround myself with good guys, but it's because most of us want to be a good dad. The enemy wants to steal the joy of being a father. Faith, hope, and love are the most excellent tools to overcome the enemy.

Faith is the evidence of things unseen, which include all the stuff we do for our kids that no one sees or recognizes. Believing in the power of God's mercy in our life brings hope. Just by reading this book there is hope because desire is the fuel for success. As we love the shame and fear off of our children, all the mistakes will fade away.

I am committed to making mistakes as loud as I can, cleaning up after, and loving my kids through their messes. It's our example as sons of Abba that will free our kids to become amazing adults. We got this!

> I am approved by God because I am His Son.

CHAPTER 15

UNBROKEN

FOR NOTHING WILL BE
IMPOSSIBLE WITH GOD.
LUKE 1:37

The term unbroken is an impossible statement. Once something is broken, it cannot be "un" broken. It can be fixed, or it can be used for some other purpose, but it can't be undone. God does the impossible. We are not to remain broken, wounded people who are doing our best. Jesus died and then was resurrected. It is impossible, yet that is what we believe. The lame walk, the blind see, the lepers are cleansed, and the dead are raised. This is the God that we believe in. The God of the impossible.

God doesn't fix things, he restores them. He makes them new. Even the covenant he made with us is new. First Corinthians chapter fifteen, verse twenty-two says, "For as in Adam all die, so also in Christ all will be made alive." We were made alive!

I was a broken man. Sitting there crying on the curb just down the street from my house; I was broken. Trying as hard as I could to control my temper it was agreed that I would leave the house instead of yelling again and causing more wounds.

All I could think about was how can I ever be the dad that I wanted to be. It was a lifelong dream to be a father, and here I was messing up my kids.

Head hung low, and tears streaming down my face, I could only utter the phrase, "help Jesus." I wanted to be the man I know God wants me to be, the dad that my kids need me to be, and the husband my wife deserves. But, how?

The lie that I was broken had soaked into every part of my being. The wounds of my life had shaped me into the person I was at that moment, but it's not the guy that God created. It was the man that I had created. I was self-made and living a life of my own design. Struggling under my own power to be self-sufficient, I had failed yet again.

I was told to, "keep failing forward." And, "It's only failure if I give up." "That which doesn't kill me makes me stronger. Suck it up. Dig deep and work harder. Someday my kids will appreciate all the hard work." Ha! I have to laugh at those lies.

Failure is a sign that we have not joined our will with the will of the Father. If there is no fruit, then we are not connected to the vine. "Abide in Me, and I in you. As the branch cannot bear fruit of itself unless it abides in the vine, so neither can you unless you abide in Me. I am the vine, you are the branches; he who abides in Me and I in him, he bears much fruit, for apart from Me you can do nothing. John 15:4-5." Yeah! Striving is a fruit of the old covenant. Jesus made a way for us to have connected lives to the Father where we bear much fruit, just by being.

We are men, made in the image of God. We were born into a world of sin and brokenness. But, by the power of the sacrifice and resurrection of Jesus, we are born again into a new covenant where all sin was paid for, and all those broken are made new.

We were created in the image of God. He didn't mess up when he made any of us. We were created perfect, and in the course of life, we are being perfected by Love. God is love. So, we are formed in the image of Love and are made perfect by Love. The fact that we were born into a fallen world, to parents that had their own issues, doesn't disqualify us from stepping into the destiny for which we were called. We are not re-made in his image. We are a new creation, made perfect.

Just about everyone I meet has some brokenness with their

father. For husbands, this is a double whammy because the man feels broken and the woman is also daddy wounded. Take two wounded people and it's no surprise that marriages are wrought with emotional pain. Add in kids, and there's the trifecta; a man with father issues has a helper with daddy wounds and is now wounding his own children because wounded people, wound people.

God is calling us men into our destiny. This is our opportunity, to break the cycle. In the old covenant, we ate of the fruit of our labors by the sweat of our brow. In the new covenant, we eat at God's banqueting table that he sets in the presence of our enemy.

Hurt people, hurt people. It's no wonder that things are getting worse and not better. The big surprise for me is that it's not much better in the church. Jesus announced that He came to bind up the brokenhearted and to proclaim freedom to the captives. Yet we still deal with father wounds, divorce, and brokenness. We are either, not teaching the liberty of the gospel correctly, or, our leaders are still so wounded that they have trouble modeling true freedom.

Once again, here is our opportunity, to walk in peace, power, and freedom as was God's design from the beginning. Wherever there isn't peace, seek the Prince of Peace. Where ever we lack the power to overcome, seek the Overcomer. If feeling trapped or stuck seek Jesus who set us free just for freedom's sake. It's time to stop trying to go at this on our own. The self-made man is killing us, wounding our children and destroying marriages. From now on be a Godmade man and seek truth and the one truth giver. Jesus said, "I am the way, and the truth, and the life; no one comes to the Father but through Me."

NOW THAT WE ARE UNBROKEN

The God of the impossible has made it possible for us to thrive.

Third John chapter 1 verse 2 says, *"Beloved, I pray that in all respects you may prosper and be in good health, just as your soul prospers."* Our call is to prosper in all respects.

What an amazing call to greatness; to prosper in every area of life. Thinking about all the areas of my life I can rate them from one to ten. How prosperous do I feel in my business, relationships, family, health, or spirit? Maybe I feel very strong at the moment, but how prosperous is cardio? What if I feel like a good father to my older kids, but still need work with the younger ones?

This is not some magic checklist that we can fill out at a seminar then go home feeling good about 80% of our lives. If we break down every aspect of what we call life, there are microcosms that we get to prosper in. Maybe my business is doing really well, but the people who work there hate their jobs.

The call to prosper is a call to become the man that we want to be. We are free to choose how far it goes. How deep in our life do we want to prosper? Take it one step at a time, or go all in, it's really up to us.

What it comes down to is this, to embrace a lie or the word of the Lord. There is no middle ground. We only get one chance at life. There is no opportunity to go back and do things over. Fortunately, we have the grace of God in our lives which empowers us to be great. The world needs us to be Godmade men.

WE ARE ONE

We are not alone. We don't need to do this by ourselves. If you suffer, I suffer. If you rejoice, I rejoice. John seventeen, eleven says, *"I will remain in the world no longer, but they are still in the world, and I am coming to you. Holy Father, protect them by the power of your name, the name you gave me, so that they may be one as we are one.* "The strength of a man is unbelievable. He can endure alone amazing amounts of suffering. Put two men together, and their power is more than double. Make them three, and now they are unstoppable. A three-chord strand is not easily broken.

There is no reason to be a man on an island of our own making. We don't need to be a husband alone. It's not a requirement to go at it alone. We are the body of Christ, unified in Him. After Peter had denied being a disciple of Christ, Jesus asks if he loves Him. Peter answers, "Yes Lord, you know that I love you." Jesus said, "feed my sheep." As Christian men, we are called to be unified in Him. My job is to examine myself (Galatians 6) so that I can be valuable to the Body of Christ.

It's not a challenge to become a better man. I don't believe that there is such a thing. Our identity is perfectly created men who are perfected in Love (God). We are everything God needs us to be. Our behaviors and actions are a different story. The mess we make is of our own design and is circumstantial evidence for our identity. That is why we examine ourselves so that our actions and behaviors are congruent with Godmade men.

Every time a man cheats on his wife, it's to our detriment. When a father is abusive to his children, it affects us all as men. On the other side, every time a man acts heroic, or protects his children or saves a life, it's to our benefit. Since we are Christians, it is double for us. When a brother falls, it affects us. When we see a good dad, it adds to us as a body.

"Beloved, I pray that in all respects you may prosper and be in good health, just as your soul prospers. (3 John 1:2)." We want to champion each other into greatness. It's for His honor that we help each other and encourage one another. We are not called to go at this alone.

Celebrate each other's victories. Don't highlight each other's failures. Support each man of God as if they were your own flesh and blood. We are made one in him and are made perfect by love. Let's show the world what Godmade men look like.

I am one with the
God of the impossible.

What am I believing about my life that feels too far gone for God?

What does the Holy Spirit have to say about this?

CHAPTER 16

THE CHANGE

BUT YOU ARE GOD'S CHOSEN TREASURE—PRIESTS WHO ARE KINGS, A SPIRITUAL "NATION" SET APART AS GOD'S DEVOTED ONES.
1 PETER 2:9

Here's where the rubber meets the road. If you've made it this far, and you didn't just start on the last chapter, then you're ready to make a life shift. Men tell me, "the spirit is willing, but the flesh is weak." So, we're going to go through the condensed version of how to get there. If this isn't enough, I have created as many options as I can to support men in becoming Godmade and living in abundance. Check out the "Freebies" section at the end of the book.

First, we must heal. Wounded people wound people. Physical healing takes time and care, but emotional healing only takes a choice. The choice is to believe something different. Core beliefs only change through conditioning in a proper environment. An environment doesn't refer specifically to the physical environment, but if your physical environment doesn't support the new change, then something should change. Our environment has to do with the people in our lives, the books we read, the stuff we listen to, and the story we tell ourselves. In this way, what we believe also impacts our environment.

Hanging around with a bunch of friends that talk poorly about their wives aren't going to help shift a belief specifically relating to marriage. Conversely, getting a divorce isn't going to change it either; actually, it will reinforce a negative belief. Be careful when considering how to deal with the people in your life. One thing that the Bible points to is that this life is about people, and Godmen steward their relationships well.

Once you've created fertile ground for changing old beliefs, then you need to take the new thought from opinion to certainty to conviction. I do this by renewing my mind to the truth. The truth is not affected by circumstance. If someone hands you an 8-ounce glass with 4 ounces of water in it, whether that glass is half full or half empty is irrelevant to the truth. The truth is that it's still four ounces of water. Choosing to believe the best about that four ounces is a biblical principle that will serve you well, but the truth is the truth.

The truth is that God is good. In every circumstance in every way, He is still good. What beliefs do you carry that do not stand up to the truth of scripture and the character of God? Write down biblical truths and read them over and over until they become a certainty. Whenever those truths prove themselves in your life, celebrate it. Eventually, your beliefs will become convictions.

Once our convictions are in line with the truth, then our world view and perspective shifts. Our thoughts, feelings, and behaviors will fall in line with what we believe, and the results will become our desires.

The last point on this is to pray constantly through this process. Being mindful of God and a desire for his highest and best is the key to creating the appropriate environment. If someone is consistently mean to you, then ask God to give you a heart of compassion for them. The beginning and end of all things should be agape love.

TOP 5 BELIEF SHIFTS

1 My Identity - Start here. Who does God say that you are? Seek identity out in scriptures, and ask Holy Spirit to reveal it to you.

2 God's Identity - I've written a lot about Father God in here and who I believe that He is. Go on a journey for yourself to shift any incorrect beliefs about his character.

3 The Man In The Mirror - Part of our identity is the statements that we make about ourselves. Stuff like, "This always happens to me." And, "That's just who I am." Even things like, "I was born this way, I can't help it." If we listen, we may hear a lot of self-proclaiming prophecy.

4 My Wife - She is a gift from God for me. She was put in my life because God loves me. Even if we came together during a time where we were far from God, she was always part of His design for my life. If you can believe that, then you're on your way!

5 Others Behaviors - How people act is not about me. I am in charge of my actions and reactions. Can I do better? Is there something to learn about myself? Wrong actions come from self-made people. As a Godmade man, I can show Jesus to them.

Create a list of beliefs that you would like to change. Begin to create an environment for those changes, and renew your mind continually. I walk men through a program I call Be - Feel - Do where we step through Identity, Mindset, and Technique which are the three primary keys to success. The results are life changing.

GROWING OR DYING

We are either growing or dying; there is no middle ground. Either life is getting better, or it's getting worse. I was definitely dying. The marriage was going backward, and my business was struggling to hang on; not growing. My health was a disaster, we ate healthy food but I never exercised, more things hurt every year, and I was not living a healthy life physically or internally.

> The lukewarm doesn't even know they are dying.
> Revelations 3:17

Jesus didn't come to make bad people good; He came to bring dead people to life. The goal in all of this is to feel alive in every area of life. It's not good enough to do the stuff. We must be growing and the proof of growth is fruit.

Two things are worth mentioning about fruit. One is that Jesus said, "I am the vine and you are the branches and no one bears fruit apart from me." The other is that fruit doesn't just have to be on the list of spiritual fruit: peace, patience, gentleness, self-control, long suffering, etc. but it's a good place to start.

All the problems in our lives are of the enemies design. When we place blame or act the victim, we are helping him with his plan. It's time to rebuke the devourer. That can look like actually rebuking, declaring, decreeing and whatever spiritual warfare looks like to you. Or, it can be merely following God's plan. Where the light is, darkness cannot exist.

It's time to shine bright and be the light. A man passionately following his heart calling is a force to be reckoned with — no shrinking back; today is my day.

"No turning back, I've made up my mind. I'm giving all of my life this time." - Jesus Culture

THE LINE IN THE SAND

Today, draw a line in the sand. Write down everything that you feel is holding you back from being everything that you want to be.

___

___

___

___

___

___

___

___

___

Now, everything on this list requires a shift in thinking. There may be some quick, "stop that" kind of behaviors but for the most part, the change is core belief driven. Most men deal with pornography, and there is a good chance that it didn't get written down on this list for all to see. I overcame a porn addiction that started when I was very young. I want to encourage any man that feels trapped by the porn monster that the pathway out is the same as getting rid of the "anger monkey." Shift beliefs, eliminate shame and be completely honest with yourself and God. I may have the courage in the future to write a book about this topic, but for now, if you need some help, please reach out through one of our social media channels.

VISION

Create a vision of how you see a Godmade life. We practiced a little of this in the opening chapter. The basic concept is that without a clear and detailed vision for the life that we want to have it will be impossible to flourish. Every leader must have a personal vision for the people they are in charge of.

Creating a vision takes some practice to be completely honest with what we want, so it's valuable to keep a vision fluid. The main components of a viable vision is that it's no longer than three years from today, and it creates positive feelings when thinking about the outcome.

I always start with a dream that seems really far off. Dream big and think about things that seem outside the realm of possibility. Then I move on to what would be good to accomplish in the next three years that could move me toward the big dream.

Here's the key to it all; feel it. Close your eyes and think about what it would feel like to achieve each part of that vision. If the vision is owning a bed and breakfast business then think about sitting in your office running that company. What kind of mug are you drinking your coffee from? How many staff members do you have? What city is it in? Go into detail and really envision yourself in that place.

Do this for every area of life and write it down. Take the time to feel it, think about things, and envision them as a reality. What does it feel like? Write the vision down clearly and with the intention of using it as a guid to run toward destiny.

> Record the vision and inscribe it on tablets,
> that the one who reads it may run.
> -Habakkuk 2:2

_____

_____

_____

_____

_____

_____

_____

_____

_____

Now, what would it feel like if three years from today nothing changes? What does it feel like if you're in the same financial situation, your relationships and family situations are the same?

What if, nothing more was accomplished? How would that feel?

If you're anything like me, then it would feel like a waste of life. Here's the thing, three years are going to come and go one way or the other. There is never a better time than today to fulfill the calling in your heart.

ONE SHOT

Things get in the way, and life happens, but don't allow the wind and waves to distract from Jesus' calling to come and walk on water with him. If you need help, then get it. We must be open-hearted and vulnerable with our spouse and the safe people in our life.

We get one shot at life. We are this age only once. Our children are only young for a short time, and our wives will only put up with our B.S. (Belief System) for so long. Tomorrow is not guaranteed, we have only right now to become the man that we want to be. Who do I want to be? What legacy will I leave behind? When people tell the story of my life what will they say? Most importantly, when I stand before God and He tells me the story of my life, what will He say?

Now is my time. Today is the day that I step into greatness. I will never be the same. I will be a new creation. The old has passed away, and from this day forward I am a Godmade man.

Today, I step into greatness.

GODMADE MEN DECLARATIONS

1. I am created for greatness not mediocrity.
2. I am a Godmade man.
3. I am approved by God.
4. I love fearlessly as Jesus does.
5. God is involved in every part of my life.
6. My actions align with my intentions.
7. I speak with kindness and love.
8. I prove my love by actions.
9. Intimacy is a two way street.
10. I champion my family into their dreams.
11. I always choose connection when I want to disconnect.
12. My kids' behavior reflect my attitude.
13. I serve my family with joy and freedom.
14. I am approved by God because I am His Son.
15. I am one with the God of the impossible.
16. Today I step into greatness.

ABOUT THE AUTHOR

RYAN ANDREWS went from a failing marriage and a broken soul to a dream life. Through heartache and struggle he learned the hard way what a life built by his own design looks like. Now that he lets God's grace and mercy soak into every area of his life he now lives full of peace, power, and freedom.

He is a husband to the perfect woman, a father to four perfect children, and the owner of a perfect soul. He has learned the power of believing that what God says about him is true and lives in that truth. He live in Newport Beach, California and he and his wife homeschool their kids. He gets to work from home, and take these amazing people all over the world.

He is honored that God entrusted these beautiful people to him and he gives all the glory God for where they are today. It's by His design that Ryan has a joy filled marriage and happy children.

MY GIFT TO YOU

SHARING IS CARING PROGRAM

Share this book with anyone that you want by sending them this link. We'll cover the cost of the book, and you cover the cost of shipping and handling.

Godmade.men/book

GODMADE MEN: The Making

It's a group of men who are not willing to settle for average marriages and families. Everyone who is a part of this group, genuinely wants to be everything that GOD MADE them to be.

Weekly – challenges, networking, training, motivation, collaboration, and more!

Get your first month free!
Godmade.men/themaking-promo

GODMADE MEN COACHING

Schedule a free 20 min chat with us!
Godmade.men/coach

GODMADE MEN'S GROUP

Godmade.men/fbgroup

GET THE PODCAST

Godmade.men/podcast

THE MAKING

JOIN OUR GODMADE MEN MASTERMIND

Godmade Men: The Making is a live, online, mastermind community of men who are not willing to settle for average marriages, families, churches, and businesses. It's God's design to get small groups of men together to create MASSIVE action. "As iron sharpens iron, so one person sharpens another." We become the man of our calling; together. Not every guy needs to work on their fitness, and not every guy needs to work on their marriage. We've designed the community with specific rooms to allow growth in whatever area you are most interested in that week. We have five rooms each week. Join one or join all, but come and be made by God.

Growth Room:

- Group Life Coaching: There is no more effective way to get unstuck than in a group of guys getting over their junk.
- Dreams and Purpose: Find purpose & live your dreams

Family Room:

- Marriage: Love every second of your marriage and have sex like newlyweds.
- Parenting: Open discussion about what works and what doesn't.

Kingdom Room:

- Healing: If you're in pain or sick or want to pray for others, join us.
- Prophetic Time: We all are Godmade men in the making, so this is a safe place to get a prophetic word and practice giving prophetic words.
- Bible Study: This is all about what God is speaking to us through scripture.

- Power Prayer: There is nothing more important than having a strong prayer life. We pray together for our wives, children, jobs, nation, or whatever God brings to us.

Business Room:
- Leadership: Kingdom based leadership, what does it look like to lead teams, inside the church and in businesses.
- Legacy Investing: We have a wealth of knowledge in our community from real estate to crypto currency to traditional channels.
- Entrepreneurship: Start a new business, grow your current one, get marketing tips, and other support and learning.

Body Room:
- Health: Let's get healthy together! I've been living healthy since I was a little kid. The wealth of knowledge that will be poured out in this room through myself and other amazing people will not want to be missed.
- Fitness: Everyone's journey is different, but we can all learn from each other. Join challenges, get WOD's, and support each other.
- Weight Loss: We go through the psychology of permanent weight loss, discuss the pros and cons of different diets, and have monthly challenges.

We do live mastermind discussions every week day in one of the rooms. If you can't make it live, the replay will be available.

APPLY NOW
https://godmade.men/themaking

www.ingramcontent.com/pod-product-compliance
Lightning Source LLC
Chambersburg PA
CBHW060534100426
42743CB00009B/1531